LEADERSHIP IN A SUCCESSFUL PARISH

LEADERSHIP
IN A
SUCCESSFUL
PARISH

Thomas P. Sweetser, S.J.
Carol Wisniewski Holden

1817

HARPER & ROW, PUBLISHERS, SAN FRANCISCO

Cambridge, Hagerstown, New York, Philadelphia, Washington
London, Mexico City, São Paulo, Singapore, Sydney

FIRST EDITION

Library of Congress Cataloging-in-Publication Data

Sweetser, Thomas P.
  Leadership in a successful parish.

  1. Pastoral theology—Catholic Church. 2. Catholic Church—Clergy. 3. Christian leadership. I. Holden, Carol Wisniewski. II. Title.
BX1913.S93   1987   253   86-45386
ISBN 0-06-254065-3 (pbk.)

88 89 90 91 MPC 10 9 8 7 6 5 4 3 2

To Carol's husband and parents
for their support and encouragement
during her years of ministry to parishes,

and in memory of
Tom's sister, Marion Garvey,
a parish minister who was without guile.

CONTENTS

FIGURES

FOREWORD

James Dunn, in *Jesus and the Spirit: A Study of the Religious and Charismatic Experience of Jesus and the First Christians as Reflected in the New Testament* (Philadelphia: The Westminster Press, 1975), expresses a preference for Paul's vision of Church. This is a vision of a community of many charisms unified by the Spirit of Christ and in dynamic tension with apostolic authority, the kerygmatic tradition, and total well-being of all the people. Dunn is not alone in his preference. The values of this vision (not its dated particularities) have been retrieved by many in the contemporary Church.

Those who have tried to enact this vision would also understand from the inside Dunn's further remarks. "Whether his [Paul's] vision was ever realized for any period of time we cannot tell. . . . It may be unworkable in practice, so deeply does the inner contradiction within individual believers run that it prevents the sort of mutual interaction that Paul envisages as the functioning of charismatic community" (p. 360). With this monumental difficulty stated in so intimidating a fashion, we are then treated to a "Where shall we go, you have the words of eternal life?" (Jn. 6:68) sentiment. "But the alternatives [to Paul's vision] suffer from even graver weaknesses and are exposed to more serious dangers, so that the Pauline vision retains its attractiveness" (p. 360).

Damned if we do, and damned if we don't. If we do not pursue the Pauline vision, even greater dangers await us. If we do pursue the vision, there is no guarantee that it is not intrinsically unworkable.

This double damnation is often what frustrated local Church leadership feels. The Catholic Church in general and the local parish in particular are in transition from a hierarchical to a community model. This means not that one model replaces the other, but that the values of both models are held in tension so that the mission of the Church can be carried on more effectively. Ideally, the values of the Pauline vision—recognition of diversity of gifts, service, mutuality, cooperation, emphasis on the local church— interact with the values of the hierarchical model—direction, authority, correction, emphasis on the universal church—to create a new embodiment of the Church in history.

The attractive vision of this new synthesis of the elements of Catholic ecclesiology awaits the practical knowledge and skills to make it work. It is admirable to dream a dream, but it is frustrating to dream a dream that has no hope of even partial realization. Theologians are fond of saying, ''Where vision fades, the people perish.'' But there is an equally high-flying banner, ''Where vision flourishes and skills flounder, the people perish.'' The dreamer and the practioner have to come together. The criticism that leaders ''can't see beyond their own noses'' is matched by the criticism that they ''would goof up a one-horse funeral.''

Perhaps an overly sophisticated way of stressing the need for a combination of vision and tactic is to recognize that modern consciousness is differentiated. We can approach life from a biological, psychological, sociological, political, or theological perspective. What is most needed in the Church at the present moment seems to be a combination of psychosocial and theological perspectives. In this way the ultimate convictions of faith and values merge with more immediate forms of analysis and action. In this scenario theology is saved from the ivory tower, and the psychosocial perspective, which has a tendency to go off on its own, is informed by the deepest instincts of faith.

This is precisely where Thomas Sweetser and Carol Wisniewski Holden come in. They provide the immediate analysis and suggest the practical skills needed to realize a contemporary ecclesial vision. *Leadership in a Successful Parish* is what I call a ''get smart'' book. Let's get smart about the functional and symbolic role of pastor, how the pastor relates to staff and the staff to council, how multiple ministries come together to make the parish work, how a staff struggles to become a team, and how leadership and people work together. In other words, let's use the forms of analysis and skills from organizational development, sociology, and psychology to serve the development of local Church communities.

Leadership in a Successful Parish is a contemporary book of proverbs—observations on experience which, if heeded, promise more successful parishes. There is practical wisdom on every page. The explicit ecclesiology can be read between the lines. In terms of the universal-local tension of Catholic ecclesiology, *Leadership in a Successful Parish* focuses on the parish and its subunits. But it does this with the realization that only an effectively organized grassroots community can incorporate the universal dimension of Church. In terms of the community-mission tension of Catholic ecclesiology, it focuses on the community's internal relationships. But it does this with the recognition that the health of the community is the indispensible prerequisite for the carrying out of the mission. In other words, the overall enterprise of Church is presupposed. What is explored with a good deal of moxie are the nitty-gritty interactions that either make parishes work or bring them to grinding halts.

Leadership in a Successful Parish is filled with concrete procedures and practical ideas. But for me an added bonus is the consistent exposure to a specific way of thinking. What this book reveals is a *habitus* of mind, a way of perceiving, analyzing, and acting attentively to the complexity of people and the diversity of detail. A careful reading can communicate this style as well as the particular ideas.

The old adage is: "Don't give people fish; teach them how to fish." Tom Sweetser and Carol Wisniewski Holden do both. They give us some fine ideas and they teach us how to think for ourselves.

The Rev. John Shea

PREFACE

This book is a result of many threads of thoughts and experiences that have been woven into a single theme of parish leadership. Leadership itself has many facets. Focusing on the abilities, talents, styles, and personality of the leaders is not enough. Other aspects must be included for a complete understanding of leadership.

The people, for instance, affect how the leaders behave. The group's expectations, desires, background, experience, and expertise exert pressure on the leader's style, changing it to fit the needs of the group. Environment also plays a role. The same leader and group will behave differently in a relaxed setting with soft chairs and indirect lighting than in a work-oriented atmosphere with tables and straight-backed chairs.

A fourth aspect of leadership is (S)spirit. This word has been spelled with both a large and a small *s* to show that the Holy Spirit plays a vital role in parish leadership. Sometimes the most well-planned meeting or program fails, while another parish event, one that did not receive much attention from the leaders, results in a large turnout and unexpected praise from the parish community as a whole. It is the Spirit at work, showing where changes or new emphases are needed. Leadership also is affected by the spirit of the group. Past experiences or present influences affect the way the leaders and people interact. The time of day, the season of the year, the weather outside, or the group climate inside can change the spirit of both leaders and people and influence the outcome. The way these four aspects of leadership—leader, people, environment, and spirit—are played out in a parish is the subject matter of this book.

Another major impetus for this book is our experience in the Parish Evaluation Project (PEP). Thomas Sweetser founded PEP in 1973. Since that time PEP has worked with over one hundred parishes throughout the United States for extended periods, up to three years in some cases. The PEP members spend at least two years in an individual parish, helping the leadership survey parishioners' attitudes and expectations, focus limited resources to meet needs uncovered by the survey, establish long-range goals and future directions, strengthen leadership skills, reorganize parish structures, and evaluate liturgies and programs to reflect parish priorities and emphases.

A shift took place in 1980 when Carol Wisniewski Holden joined PEP. The two of us try, through many peaks and valleys, to work as a team. The effort continues to this day as we work with parishes, teach classes, conduct workshops, and give talks on parish ministry. Our personal experience of team ministry and our first-hand exposure to a wide variety of parish situations have led to this collaborative writing effort.

Besides this background in parish research and development, two specific experiences led to this book. One was Carol's decision to enroll in a Doctorate of Ministry program sponsored by St. Mary of the Lake Seminary of the Chicago Archdiocese. After completing two years of course work, she decided to focus on parish staff team building as the subject of her thesis. The second experience was an invitation Tom received from James Alt Publishers to write a weekly column on parish ministry for diocesan newspapers throughout the country. The column began in September 1983 and concluded in August 1984. The material from Tom's columns and Carol's team-building process form the background of *Leadership in a Successful Parish*.

One last occasion served to nudge us into action and started us writing in earnest. A group of Chicago area pastors was becoming concerned about the low morale among Catholic priests, especially among pastors. The job of pastoring was causing stress and tension, with little relief in sight. They approached the Parish Evaluation Project for help. The result was an article that appeared in the April 1985 issue of *Chicago Studies*, "The Problems and Promise of Being Pastor." We are grateful to the editor of *Chicago Studies*, Rev. George Dyer, for granting permission to reprint this article as

Chapter 2 in this book. We would also like to thank the editors of *Upturn*, the monthly publication of the Association of Chicago Priests, for permission to reprint the case study that appears in Chapter 4.

Many others have helped us in the creation of this work. For instance, the many pastors, staffs, councils, and parish leaders we have worked with in recent years have contributed a great deal to the book's content and emphases. To these parish ministers, too many to mention by name, we are grateful.

We wish to thank by name a few people who have helped in this effort. Bernadette Scalzitti helped with the preparation of the manuscript. Jim and Evelyn Whitehead, Linda Maser, Tom Holden, Kate and Dick Hage, Janice Klein, Cheryl Furtak, and Jim Ewens lent their support, and they offered helpful suggestions on the final draft. We give special thanks to Rev. John Shea for his contribution in writing the Foreward.

Chapter 1

PARISH: AT THE CROSSROADS

One day, not so long ago, the leaders from Holy Family parish attended a diocesan workshop on parish ministry. They listened to the speakers, divided up into interest groups, picked up literature on new programs and books on ministry, and left the meeting wondering what this had to do with their own rather pitiful situation. They were feeling discouraged and weighed down because the workshop uncovered some of the weaknesses of their parish. They sought out others to talk with about their frustrations.

The pastor went out to dinner with a few of his classmates. They felt they needed a reward for attending the workshop. They had been "requested" by the bishop to attend and from what the speakers and group leaders were saying, the priests did not feel they received much in the way of reward or support for their efforts at pastoring.

The pastor and his four companions spent the evening sharing their thoughts about being pastor in a modern Catholic parish. "Who needs all this grief?" the pastor of Holy Family began. "Nothing I do is right. My staff is at my neck for not including them more in the decision making of the parish. The council, which is really a waste of time, keeps complaining about my laid-back style. I get so frustrated because I'm trying to give them the responsibility, but they lay it right back in my lap. The committees of the council are a joke. The only one that is working is the education committee, but they are running into opposition from the school board. Both groups come running to me to solve their problems." The other three pastors nodded in agreement and told similar stories about their own parishes.

At the same moment, in another, somewhat less pretentious restaurant across town, the young associate from the parish was talking over his experience with his own classmates. "It was a good workshop today," he began, "but it won't amount to a hill of beans at our parish. For one thing, the boss is just hanging on till he can get a small parish with no school, no staff, and no hassles. The only way I can survive is to stay out of the way. The pastor is so noncommittal that I never know where he's coming from. I've just carved out my little niche with the choir, young adults, and prayer groups and let him handle the rest.

"And the staff meetings, for my money, are a waste of time. Those two women who run the religious education programs are out to get me, I swear. They think I need changing so I won't be so clerical, but it's the only way I can keep my sanity at our staff meetings. Those two want to take over the parish. They have almost succeeded with their education committee."

His classmates chided him for being a woman hater and a Romanizer, but they went easy on him because they knew he was hurting. They wondered what was happening to their old friend. He was more bitter and cynical of late.

The two women on the parish staff stayed behind for the potluck dinner that followed the workshop. They had brought dishes and found the sharing of food and conversation with other staffs helpful. They were somewhat miffed that the priests chose not to stay and share the meal, but they were not surprised. It was to be expected. They picked up their meal and sat down with a few other religious education coordinators and started to swap stories.

"This was a good workshop," one of them said. "All that good information on team building, shared decision making, and staff collaboration. But will it do any good? I doubt it. I was watching my pastor during that section on conflict management. It didn't even faze him. What does one do? We've decided to spend our energies on our own education committee and see if that model might affect other areas of the parish. We're helpless to do anything directly. Oh, we've tried, but the priests hold all the cards—aces, trump, long suits—all we have are a couple of deuces."

"We had such hopes when the new pastor came," the other woman added. "He looked like the perfect successor to our previous pastor, who was such a good team player. But, instead, we get a laissez-faire, noncommital person who just lets the whole thing go its own way. We're not sure how long we can last.''

The rest of the people at the table listened in silence, wondering how to help these two.

Holy Family's permanent deacon was unable to attend the bi-weekly staff meetings but did have a chance to take in this ministry workshop. He went home to talk over the experience with his wife. It was not a new conversation, but one they had often. She herself was active in the parish, and the two of them were concerned about rising tensions.

The deacon and his wife agreed that the pastor and associate didn't seem to be talking to each other, and it showed in the weekend liturgies. Each did his own thing, and it was confusing to the people: both presiders read the announcements at different times; the pastor used the book prepared by the liturgy committee, but the associate refused to do so. Each priest was accummulating a follow-ing, so it was beginning to appear that there were two parishes instead of one. Further complicating matters, the two women on staff were getting more and more bitter about their secondary role. It was almost as though the parish was split into camps at war with one another. The deacon and his wife felt as if they were helpless bystanders. What could they do to help pull the parish together? Where would they turn for help?

Two women from the parish council also attended the workshop. They were amazed at all the people who came and who seemed to know what they were doing. These two felt out of place. They stopped off for a cup of coffee after the workshop to talk over the day. They were not informed about the potluck and so felt awkward staying for dinner afterwards.

As they drank their coffee, they complained to each other about no one telling them what was going on—the potluck being the most recent example. They felt in the dark about their role on the council. There was such a contrast between their own experience and what was talked about at the workshop.

''For one thing,'' one of the women remarked, ''I had no prepa-ration for this council business. Father called me up and said he wanted me to run for the council, and that was it. The election was a farce because no one ran against me, and only a small portion of the parish bothered to vote. The monthly meetings are disasters with no agenda, purpose, or direction. No wonder people come late, if at all.

"I'm not a quitter, but this thing is driving me batty. And what did we hear today? 'The council is to share the leadership role with pastor and staff.' That I'd like to see. We could dissolve the council, and it wouldn't make a bit of difference. Nor would the parish either care or even realize it was gone. Joyce, why are we doing this to ourselves?"

These reflections from Holy Family's leadership are fictitious, made up from our experience of Catholic parishes in recent years. We would like to think that this is a rare and unusual occurrence, but it is not. The pastor is ill-equipped for his role. He assumes that shared decision making means giving up all claim to pastoral leadership. The associate feels left out and inadequate, so he retires to a safe distance and loses himself in isolated areas of pastoral ministry.

The two women staff members feel unsupported and alienated from a parish and Church suspicious of their talents, training, and pastoral ambitions. The deacon is unsure why he was ordained or what his role is. The council has been called into existence to provide help and direction to the priests and staff in leading the parish. For the present, however, they amount to only a burden and an obstacle to parish growth.

This book offers ways out of the malaise in which Holy Family finds itself. For each area of parish leadership, suggestions and aids for developing effective and productive leadership in a successful parish are presented.

The History of the Parish

The American Catholic parish is in the midst of a *paradigm shift*. Scientists use that term to describe leaps in the understanding and ordering of scientific knowledge. The old explanations of nature do not hold up. New terms must be used to explain the present phenomenon. The leap from Newtonian physics to quantum mechanics and relativity is an example of such a paradigm shift.

A similar paradigm shift is happening in Catholic parishes, especially among the leaders. An entirely new reality is upon us. The old explanations and descriptions no longer hold up. The parish is at a most critical moment in its history. It is at a crossroads and the path chosen will decide the future of the parish.

The origins and development of parish life provide a perspective for judging the present situation and future directions. Parishes did not begin until the fourth century. For the first few centuries after Christ, the Church thrived in small groups, such as homes, catacombs, and small churches, presided over by the local bishop. It was a vital, growing Church and the people had a close connection with the head of the community, the bishop.[1]

By the fourth century most Christians were clustered around a central worship center (basilica). Some, however, lived at a distance from the place of worship, and the leaders were concerned about those who could not get to the bishop's Mass. We have evidence from the correspondence of Pope Celasius I (492–496) that the solution to this problem was to divide up the rural areas into parishes, each of which was placed under the jurisdiction of a resident priest (presbyter). The pope's correspondence dealt with the correct disposition of the parish's revenues. He stipulated that one-fourth of the revenue should go to the upkeep and maintenance of the parish, one-fourth to the poor and dependents, one-fourth to the pastor, and one-fourth to the bishop.

It is not clear where the revenues to support these parishes came from. At least some of the income came from the celebration of the solemn sacraments of baptism, weddings, and funerals. Revenue also came from the land attached to the parish. The amount of land varied with the locale. Only later, at the time of Charlemagne, did the size of the parish land become standardized into what was called the altar plot.

More information about the development of parish life came during the pontificate of Gregory the Great. In 591, Pope Gregory appointed two pastors and a deacon to parishes in Tuscany, Italy, instead of waiting for the usual election of the pastor by the people. Up to this time it appears that the customary procedure was to have the people choose their pastor. But beginning with Pope Gregory, bishops selected the pastors, and the appointment was for life. The pastor was also given certain duties: to perform solemn baptisms, to exact the Easter penance duty, to perform burials, and to require parishioners to attend the parish on Sundays and feast days.

In 787, the Council of Nicaea ratified these duties of a pastor and gave him further rights: the pastor could not be removed from office by the bishop, and the pastor was given title to the parish property in order to provide for his sustenance. Some pastors were "charging" too much for solemn sacraments, causing hardship and scandalizing the people. Thus, the pastor received property to provide him with an income.

The Council of Nicaea also required pastors to provide training for young clerics, beginning with tonsure and minor orders. This is the first evidence we have of schools connected with parishes. But in most cases the pastors were ineffective, and eventually the educational task was taken over by the monasteries. Many of the pastors themselves were not trained or equipped for their job, so training others was out of the question.

Most of the records of the development of the parish are the result of controversies and conflicts of interest. The correspondence arising from the management of these conflicts provides insights into the way parish life was organized. One of these conflicts was the friction that existed between parishes and local shrines. Shrines, which honored local saints and martyrs, attracted many people away from the parishes. One way of correcting this loss of membership (and revenue) was to oblige parishioners to attend Mass in the parish on Sundays and feast days.

This was the beginning of the Mass obligation. It wasn't that people failed to attend Mass, but that they were not attending Mass in the parish. Beginning in the eighth century, people were required to attend the parish Mass on Sundays and feast days. Only the pastor could release people from this obligation.

Charlemagne, at the beginning of the ninth century, played a role in parish development, more influential than the pope or any of the councils of that era. Charlemagne assured pastors of a land title amounting to about twenty acres, called the altar plot. He also exempted pastors from paying any taxes on this land. He changed the tradition for selection so that pastors were once again chosen by the people and could only be removed by means of a trial.

Although this might sound progressive and democratic, in reality it took the power of selection out of the hands of the bishop and put it into the hands of the ruling monarch. In return for this greater stability and status, pastors could no longer charge fees for solemn baptism and had to reside in only one parish. Some pastors, it appears, "owned" a number of parishes and collected revenues from the land and sacraments connected with them.

The outcome of Charlemagne's decrees on parish life was that the pastor became not only the spiritual, but also the secular leader of the area. Parishes became the place for conducting local business and exercising political power. The term *secular clergy,* applied to priests, derives from this practice. Even in the United States, Louisiana's political subsections are called parishes rather than counties.

Following Charlemagne's reign parishes experienced a period of decline during the Dark Ages. The decline continued until the thirteenth century. As a result charismatic individuals and groups sought to fill the vacuum. A number of religious orders were founded during this period. But with the rise of these orders came inevitable clashes between the secular clergy and religious orders.

Pope Sixtus IV (1471–1481) tried to manage these conflicts by setting down the following guidelines:

1. Masses offered by the religious orders satisfied the people's obligation to attend Mass on Sundays and feasts days.
2. Bishops had control over the list of approved confessors. Priests had to have "faculties" in order to hear confession. This provided some control over the activities of religious orders in a diocese.
3. Charitable institutions were separated from parishes so that religious orders could care for the physical needs of people independent of the pastors.
4. A pastor still had the final authority over the people under his jurisdiction and could impose censures on those who got out of line.

Pope Sixtus' guidelines, however, did not clear up the conflicts. The pontiff was unable to clarify the boundary problem: Who belonged to what parish? Where did one pastor's jurisdiction end and another's begin? This dispute continued until the Council of Trent.

The twenty-fourth session of the Council of Trent, held in 1563, addressed parish life and organization in the following ways:

1. Clarified parish boundaries so that every parish within a diocese had a territorial definition. This stipulation had many exceptions, however, as the ethnic, nonterritorial parishes of American cities manifest.
2. Gave pastors control over the sacraments administered to their people to such an extent that marriages performed without the pastor's consent were invalid.
3. Guaranteed pastors an income: no longer did one-fourth of the parish income go to the bishop.
4. Specified that pastors were to be selected by the bishop and had to pass an examination to show they were equipped for the job. Once appointed, they were guaranteed that pastorate for life.
5. No longer consigned the Sunday obligation for attending Mass to the local parish. Any valid Mass would do. Pastors could no longer impose censures on their people.

The Council of Trent solidified parish development for the next four centuries. A few minor changes did occur, however. During the pontificate of Clement XI (1700–1721), pastors received jurisdiction over processions and blessings. When Benedict XIV was pope, pastors who were appointed for life had to pass a written examination that was more rigorous than for temporary pastors. No longer was every pastor guaranteed the position until he died.

In 1917 the Code of Canon Law systematized the centuries of adaption and development by spelling out the duties and rights of pastors. Pastors are expected to do the following:

1. Reside in the parish and have only one parish at a time.
2. Have jurisdiction over the sacraments administered to the people.
3. Offer Masses for the people and provide for the education of the youth.
4. Perform works of mercy.

5. Administer the money of the parish under the bishop's supervision.
6. Grant dispensations to the people whenever necessary.
7. Be examined and approved by the bishop if they have been appointed for life.

Notice that the needs and rights of the parishioners are not mentioned, only alluded to in official correspondence and papal decrees. The pastor was the focus of parish life and development. While not recorded in the official documents, parishioners' initiative also shaped Church history. Take, for instance, the parishes in the colonies of the Americas during the eighteenth and nineteenth centuries. Many examples of adaption and creative initiative are evident, and these did not always include the pastor or bishop.

For example, a German congregation in the 1850's that had no pastor built a church, established a parish, and then sought a suitable priest. Once one was found—that is, one who could speak German—he was hired and paid a salary for his ministry. The bishop, of course, was informed. Because the bishop was burdened with so many problems associated with an expanding, missionary Church, he was happy to know that at least some of his flock were being cared for. In effect the congregation owned the parish and hired or fired the pastor. This practice, called trusteeism, caused many headaches for the United States' hierarchy, beginning with John Carroll, the United States' first bishop. But it did offer a creative solution to a local problem of providing pastoral care to the people. Eventually the "problem" was solved by bishops taking stronger control of the parish and placing parish financial resources under their own jurisdiction. The local bishop became the "corporate sole" or financial owner of all parishes in his diocese.

Another example of people's independence and creativity in the immigrant Church of the United States was a New York parish in lower Manhattan. A group of immigrants from Sicily took over a three-story storefront in their neighborhood. They gutted the building and built a beautiful church within, leaving no indication from the outside that it was now a church. The people found a few Sicilian Jesuits to staff their parish. Once their church was established, the people announced to the archbishop that they were a parish in his archdiocese.

Then came the Second Vatican Council. No immediate change was apparent in parish life, except by way of anticipation and apprehension. But the parish was ripe for change. The explosion began around 1967 and continued through the 1970s. The Mass changed from Latin to the venacular. People other than priests distributed Communion. Parish councils were formed, new staff positions created, women appeared in the sanctuary as lectors and commentators. Liturgical music shifted from traditional hymns to contemporary songs accompanied by guitars, flutes, and piano.

The Parish Today

The history of parish growth did not follow a predictable, unified pattern. Instead, it became localized because it was dependent upon the pastor. If the pastor was creative, sensitive, and facilitating, then parish growth happened. If he was not, then little growth occurred. Parish was synonymous with pastor.

But this may no longer be the situation in the modern parish. The change is subtle but radical in its implications. Ever since its origins, with few exceptions, the parish has belonged to the pastor. There is no question that the pastor is still an important figure in parish life and development, but does he still "own" the parish? Yes, in some parishes, to varying degrees he does, but the ownership is shifting slowly but inevitably to the parishioners. The implication of this shift—a paradigm shift—lies at the heart of what a parish is and how it is led.

Evidence of this shift is contained in the 1983 Code of Canon Law. Compare, for instance, the definition of parish in the new code with the one contained in the 1917 Code of Canon Law. In the 1917 Code of Canon Law, parish was defined as a benefice or a structure for the support of the clergy in order that services could be provided for God's people. The pastor's role was emphasized. In Canon 515 of the 1983 Code, parish is defined as a "definite community of the Christian faithful which is established on the stable basis within a particular church."[2] The emphasis has shifted from pastor to people.

The emphasis on boundaries has changed as well. No longer is territory an essential ingredient of parish, as it was for many centuries. Instead, Canon 518 of the 1983 Code reads "personal parishes should be established based upon rite, the language, or even nationality of the Christian faithful within some territory, *or even upon some other determining factor*. [emphasis added].[3]

As for leadership, the pastor is still given a prominent place, but he may not be the only leader in the parish. It is true that every parish must have a pastor who is a priest, but a pastor may be assigned to one or several parish communities. This breaks a tradition going back to the time of Charlemagne. The 1983 Code of Canon Law states in Canons 517 and 526 that a priest can be a pastor of several parishes with the daily pastoral ministry entrusted to others, such as a deacon, a vowed religious, or a trained professional minister.[4] The emphasis has shifted away from the pastor and toward the community because, above all else, the needs of the parish community are the reason for the presence of the pastor.

The 1983 Code of Canon Law also states that all the members of the parish community have a responsibility for the life and action of the parish. Parishioners are to assume this responsibility by making their views known, by sharing in the ministry, and by permeating the temporal order with a Christian spirit. The entire parish community is to work with the pastor in proclaiming the Word of God, in teaching and preparing people for reception of the Sacraments, in planning for the future through a parochial pastoral council, and in handling the temporal affairs of the parish through a body of financial advisors.[5]

The 1983 Code of Canon Law, in other words, legitimates a shift of emphasis from the pastor to the people, a shift initiated by the Second Vatican Council and developed in Catholic parishes over the last twenty years.

At the present moment American Catholic parishes stand at the crossroads. It's an uncharted and unknown journey that lies ahead. There are no precedents, no lived experience, no long-standing traditions to build upon. But certainly, leadership will critically determine whether a parish moves forward or settles back into a secure and unimaginative routine. Leadership is no longer synonymous with pastor. As the 1983 Code of Canon Law suggests, others share the leadership role with the pastor. But he still plays a critical role. It is possible for a parish to grow and develop despite the poor leadership of the pastor, but it is very difficult. For this reason our discussion of parish leadership emphasizes the pastor, both the problems he faces and the potential he has for setting the parish on the right road toward a meaningful future.

NOTES

1. For more information on the history of parishes before Vatican II, see C.J. Nuesse and Thomas J. Harte, CSSR, *The Sociology of Parish* (Milwaukee: Bruce Publishing Co., 1950).
2. Canon Law Society of Great Britain and Ireland, *The Code of Canon Law in English Translation* (London: Collins, 1983), p. 92.
3. Ibid., p. 93.
4. Ibid., p. 93-94.
5. Ibid., p. 95.

Further Reading

Cooke, Bernard. *Ministry to Word and Sacraments*. Philadelphia: Fortress Press, 1976.

Fiorenza, Elisabeth Schussler. *In Memory of Her*. New York: The Crossroad Publishing Co., 1983.

O'Meara, Thomas Franklin, O.P. *Theology of Ministry*. New York: Paulist Press, 1983.

Schillebeeckx, Edward. *Ministry: Leadership in the Community of Jesus Christ*. New York: Crossroad Publishing Co., 1981.

Chapter 2

PASTOR: THE FACILITATOR

It may be true that the pastor no longer "owns" the parish, but he is still the most important person in setting the tone and direction of the parish. Think of what happens when the pastor is moved. The tone of the liturgy changes. Parish priorities shift. New emphases and directions emerge. Parishioners wonder if they will like the new pastor, if they can work with him, and if he will agree with their understanding of Church and parish.

Those who share the new pastor's values and style will come forward to offer their help and support. Those who do not will hang back, wondering where they fit in the new arrangement. If they can't fit in, then they will either wait out the new pastor, try to have him removed, or go elsewhere. This same dynamic is not present when there is a change of associates, staff, or lay leadership. But change the pastor and the parish changes, even if not to the degree it did in the past.

The Problems of Being Pastor

Because the pastor makes so much difference, many pastors today feel burdened by leadership, wondering if it is worth all the hassles and headaches. Of course, the pastor experiences many joys as well. In the parishes where the pastor, staff, council, and parish leaders work well together, it becomes evident that the people enjoy their ministry of leadership. They help create a climate of love and concern in the parish community. Much of the climate is due to the pastor's leadership abilities.

But many other pastors are not enjoying their ministry of leadership. They feel that too much is demanded of them and too little has been provided to them by way of preparation, support, or rewards. The demands come from many quarters. Staff members want the pastor to be a colleague and to participate in the development of staff into a model of community in the parish. Any attempt by the pastor to pull rank, to be the boss, or to use his power is looked upon by staff members as a clerical, hierarchical response to what they feel should be a mutual sharing of power and responsibility.

Very little in the pastor's training has prepared him for this participatory, interactive model of leadership. He feels that if he gives in to the staff's demands, he will be shirking his duty as pastor—that is, as the one who is "in charge." Most pastors lack the skills needed to deal with shared responsibility and mutual ministry. These skills include how to arrive at a consensus, how to listen, how to manage conflict, how to give feedback, and how to evaluate performance. When a pastor does not have these skills and someone else on the staff does, the pastor feels inadequate and threatened.

Pastors also experience problems with parishioners in positions of leadership. The pastoral council, for example, rather than being a help, becomes a burden. Council meetings are endless and deal with trivial matters. The organizational design of the council is too loose, the roles unclear, and the delegation of jobs and responsibilities uneven. The pastor has no alternatives to fall back on, no awareness of possible structures and options for parish organization and management. The business models that council members propose do not fit the situation. But what does? The parish is such a complex operation, and it is up to the pastor to keep it running smoothly.

Then there are the parishioners. They look to the pastor as their leader, the one who should always be available, day or night, the one who should be present at every meeting, at every special liturgy, at every parish celebration, and at every critical moment of their lives, from birth to death. People become upset if a secretary or housekeeper or, worse yet, an answering machine comes between them and their pastor.

Not only do staff, leaders, and people cause problems, but responsibility for the parish plant itself is the pastor's. The parish needs a new church, larger meeting rooms, or more offices. The school enrollment is going down, and salaries are going up. The roof leaks, the sewers are backed up, and the windows are broken. The final responsibility for these problems is the pastor's.

Where does the pastor turn for help? To the diocese? This route is often more trouble than it is worth. The personnel board tells him not to expect an associate next year because there are not enough priests to go around. The bishop sends letters regarding special collections to be read at Mass. If quotas are not met, the parish is assessed. In addition, the diocese requests the presence of the pastor at this meeting and that celebration, and this report is due and that budget must be submitted by next week. The diocese, in other words, is not always considered a supportive structure for pastoring. Nor is Rome much help. More paperwork is demanded for marriage cases; more study is demanded by the 1983 Code of Canon Law. The pastor begins to wonder if the institutional Church really understands human needs and people's lived experience.

Five Styles of Pastoring

Pastors respond to these problems in different ways. Like all human beings, they are not consistent in their responses, but five styles can be identified. First, there is the "telling" pastor. Whether traditional or progressive, the telling pastor feels he knows what is best for the parish and sees to it that his wishes are carried out. This has been an accepted approach to pastoring up until recent years and is still used in many places: "Just tell us what to do, Father, and we'll do it." It takes the people off the hook, but it also takes away their ownership of the parish. The telling style is efficient—tasks are accomplished. It can also include a great deal of delegation and sharing of jobs, but everyone knows that it is the pastor who runs the parish.

This telling style of leadership may be necessary when a new pastor arrives and the parish is in chaos and confusion. A strong hand may be needed to put order back into the parish. But the temptation is to hang on to the power long after order has been restored. It keeps people in a child-parent relationship well beyond the time when the people have grown to adulthood and can assume ownership of the parish along with the pastor.

Another difficulty with this style of pastoring is that the people in leadership positions do not accept it any more. They may try for a while to encourage the pastor to move toward a more participatory style. If they succeed, they will continue in leadership positions. If not, they will give up, leaving the pastor, once again, "in charge." He may not be aware he is exercising a telling style, or he may feel this is the only correct or legitimate way of doing his job, but eventually he will be surrounded by people who are willing to say yes to his telling approach. As a result, shared leadership and mutual ownership of the parish will have to wait for a change in pastors.

A second style is the "selling" pastor. This is a political and, in most cases, manipulative form of pastoring. Rather than telling people what they would do or how the parish should be run, the pastor tries to shape the environment and the attitudes of the people so that eventually they come around to his way of thinking. The pastor becomes a salesperson. He makes sure that everyone feels at ease and is happy with the operation of the parish. They think they have a say in the way it is run, but in reality, it is the pastor who pulls the strings. The pastor feels a new church should be built, the sanctuary remodeled, or the school closed. He bides his time, gathering supporters, and when the time is right, he sells the staff or council or people on the idea so that they think it was their idea from the beginning.

Such an approach can work for a while, but eventually people see through this tactic and begin to feel they are being used. They often react with passive resistance. Parishioners learn to anticipate the pastor's "sell job" and put up defenses. When volunteers are needed or suggestions on planning a project requested, people are nowhere to be found. Why give ideas or get involved? The pastor will get his way in the end anyway. Because the pastor's style is indirect, so is the resistance. What is left is a vacuum of leadership, and nothing gets accomplished.

The third style is the "testing" or evaluative approach to pastoring. The pastor still makes the final decisions, but only after he checks out his ideas with those affected by the decisions. He runs the staff meetings and is the ultimate authority, but the staff members feel he listens to and acts upon their views and opinions. The parishioners know that the pastor is in charge, but they also know that he is open to reactions and criticism and that no major decision will be made until they are consulted.

Suppose the Sunday collections are not keeping up with parish expenses. The pastor contacts the diocese for help. The diocesan financial planning office supplies a program for increasing contributions that stresses stewardship, financial accountability, and tithing. Rather than introducing the new plan immediately, the pastor calls together the staff, council, and finance committee to hear their views, criticisms, and suggestions. He listens to what they have to say, makes adjustments in the proposal, and then appoints a committee to carry it to completion.

This approach is more successful in the long run than the telling or selling style. It may not satisfy everyone, especially those in leadership positions who want a mutual and equal sharing of leadership, but it is more in keeping with the collegial model of the post-Vatican II Church and the democratic style of American culture.

The fourth style is an ideal that is not often achieved. This is the "joining" or participatory, consultative style of pastoring. The configuration is circular rather than hierarchical. Decisions, at least the more important ones, are reached by consensus rather than by vote or majority opinion. This may be the ideal approach, but the cost is high, both in the time required to reach a consensus and in the skills needed for making it work. Most pastors either lose patience with the time it takes or lose heart because of their lack of skills. But for those who use the "joining" style consistently, the rewards are great. The pastor is no longer the primary decision maker in the parish. As a result, the burdens of authority and sole ownership of the parish are shared with others.

In the participatory style the pastor still exercises strong leadership. However, the emphasis is not on making the final decisions, but on creating the most conducive environment and climate for people to participate in identifying the problems and choosing the best solutions. The pastor makes sure that everyone has a part to play. He establishes an appropriate process for gathering the necessary information, for helping people stay with a decision until everyone can own and accept the result, and for dividing up the work so that all are included and are given areas of co-responsibility. It can be an exciting style of pastoring, one in which everyone becomes a co-owner of the task and co-minister of the parish as a whole. But it does take skill, time, and much patience as people try to understand and practice this new approach to shared leadership of the parish.

As an example of a facilitating approach to pastoral leadership, suppose a parish's sanctuary is in need of remodeling. Twenty years ago, in response to the liturgical changes initiated by Vatican II, a temporary altar was set up and the altar rail removed. It is now time to make these changes permanent and to create a conducive atmosphere for worship. The pastor brings up the sanctuary renovation project at the weekly staff meeting. The staff agrees it is a good time to start the project. One of the staff members, the music director, volunteers to work with the pastor, and the rest of the staff lend their support and encouragement.

The next step is to assemble a special committee to gather information and generate options. Members of the council, liturgy committee, and choir agree to join the pastor and music director on the Sanctuary Renovation Committee. They meet to plan their strategy. One member of the committee, not the pastor, is selected by the group to be the coordinator. Over the next few months, the committee studies diocesan guidelines and liturgical recommendations. They consult with a number of architects and visit other churches for ideas. The pastor helps the committee locate creative options, informs them of guidelines and financial constraints, and acts as a catalyst for their task.

At the end of this informaton-gathering stage, the committee comes up with three options for the renovation, complete with a rationale for each one, diagram, and cost projections. The three options are presented to a joint meeting of the staff and council for comments and criticism. The renovation committee runs the meeting. The pastor not only participates, but also makes sure all present are contributing their ideas and feelings in a spirit of mutual trust and acceptance. At the conclusion of the meeting, the committee, staff, and council reach a consensus on which option is best. But they do not make a decision to proceed with the renovation. First, it must go the people. This is where a facilitating style of leadership is most important.

The pastor speaks at all the Masses, explaining the work of the Sanctuary Renovation Committee, the reasons for the change, and the proposed option. He invites the parishioners to pray about the option and offer reasons for and against this move. In other words, he asks the entire congregation to participate in the process. The pastor, along with the committee, listens to the people's reaction, paying close attention to emotions. The people know that in giving their reactions, they are not voting, but are allowing the desires of the Spirit to be expressed through them. The results of this listening period is a positive, supportive response from a large majority of the parishioners. Those opposed to the project know that they have been heard and are willing to go along with the renovation because it appears that this is what the Spirit is calling the parish to do and that it would be best for the community as a whole. The committee then recommends to the staff and council that the renovation be undertaken. In this style of leadership, the pastor sets the tone and facilitates rather than makes the decision himself.

The fifth approach is the "resting" or laissez-faire style of being pastor. A number of pastors, out of a desire to share the leadership of the parish, gives up all claim to being the pastor. The pastor becomes one of the group to such an extent that no one knows the purpose or direction of the parish. We also refer to this as the "crowd" style. Once the pastor decides to give up his role as pastor, the parish becomes a do-it-yourself operation, that is, a collection of projects and programs, liturgies, and activities with no connecting links. Rather than helping a parish solve its problems, set directions, or use its resources well, the laissez-faire pastor becomes a member of the crowd, expecting the parish to run itself and groups to function on their own.

Groups rarely do. They need leadership and direction—not dictatorial or manipulative leadership, but guidelines, timetables, and established parameters within which to operate. If a group knows that it has two hours to complete a task, that it has all the tools available to get the task done, and that it has alternatives and options available in case it encounters difficulties, then it can do the job. The role of the leader (in this case the pastor) is to set limits, create the right environment, supply the needed tools, skills, and processes, and offer alternatives and options when necessary. A laissez-fair pastor has given up these important leadership prerogatives. As a result, the parishioners become confused, fragmented, and angry. Parish leaders who try to operate in this laissez-faire environment either quit out of frustration or try to take over the reins so that something can get accomplished. The pastor himself, in witnessing either people's nonattendance or their power plays as they attempt to get something accomplished, panics and takes the only reasonable course of action; he becomes the boss, makes the decisions himself, and tells people what to do. The people will accept this authoritarian approach with relief. Anything is better than a leaderless parish. At least someone is taking charge. But this is just the style the pastor was trying to avoid by giving over the leadership to the group. We have, in other words, come full circle, from a telling to a resting style and back again.

The Potential of the Facilitating Style

The consultative style of pastoring provides the most promise for leadership in the American Catholic parish. But it takes different forms depending on the location, size, and type of parish served. For the six different situations that follow, we suggest the consultative, participatory style of pastoring that best fits the context.

A parish serving a primarily black population can benefit from a team approach to pastoring. In this situation the pastor would be one among equals. Perhaps a nun, a permanent deacon, and a woman parishioner would share with the pastor the professional ministry and pastoral leadership of the parish. Their role would be to act as a model of collaborative ministry to the parish and as a mutual support to one another. The priest would be a co-pastor along with other team members. He probably would not be black himself, but would learn from the others on the team and from the parishioners what it is like to be a black Catholic in today's society and in the Church. His pastoring would be both receptive and facilitating.[1]

Much the same approach is necessary in pastoring an Hispanic parish. The pastor must be both student and teacher. As a student he must learn Spanish, accept Hispanic customs and piety, and build on Hispanic traditions and insights into human nature. The pastor must be able to create and foster small group discussions or "base communities" that provide parishioners with opportunities to tell their own stories about the joys and difficulties of fitting into an alien culture and unfamiliar church. Storefront churches and fundamental sects have had great success relating to the needs and desires of Hispanics. Effective pastoring to an Hispanic community demands an awareness of what draws people to other churches and what similar opportunities might be offered in the Catholic parish.

Pastoring in a large, urban parish with predominantly older, more traditional Catholics demands special skills, as well as much patience. The people, most of whom have been members of the parish for many years, treasure traditions practiced over the years. At the same time the people often have an underlying fear of change, especially change in the surrounding neighborhood. The people are afraid for their own safety, for their future, and of disruptions in their familiar routine. Pastoring in this environment demands insight into what is likely to happen in the area, including patterns of growth and decline and ethnic shifts.

Once the future directions are discovered, the pastor must prepare the older people for the changes and make room for the newer groups moving into the area. Some of the skills required are (1) gathering information, (2) reading the signs of change, (3) helping people vent their feelings and fears, (4) listening patiently to people's stories and past experiences, (5) giving people new visions and hope for a manageable future, and (6) sharing good humor so that people can still celebrate the lighter side of parish life. The pastor does not have to have all these skills himself, but he must gather around him those who do. In this way the parishioners begin to see the changes as opportunities for growth rather than as precursors of death and decline.

Being a pastor in a suburban area with young parishioners requires a different set of skills. This environment requires strong leadership, but not of the authoritarian kind. The parishioners are well educated and work in responsible occupations requiring leadership abilities, equipping them to plan and accomplish tasks. At the same time they are overextended, struggling to make ends meet while raising a family. As a result they have little time left over for parish involvement. Pastoring in this setting demands (1) focusing energies, (2) making the best use of people's time, and (3) helping parishioners use their talents and abilities without wearing them out in the process. The greatest danger, both to staff and parishioners, is burnout. The pastor must create the most conducive environment so that people's talents and abilities can be utilized for parish growth without overburdening himself and other leaders.

If a generous person volunteers for a job, the pastor does not give the person six other tasks at the same time. If a staff member is willing to take on a new project, the pastor suggests the person drop another job to make room for the new one. If a meeting is to last until ten in the evening, the pastor sees to it that it stops on time or even a little early. Channeling people's energy and setting limits is the key to good pastoring in a young, suburban parish.

In an older, well-established, more affluent suburb, another emphasis might be necessary. In this case the people have settled into a home, business, and routine. The temptation is to look to the parish as one of many status symbols. The pastor becomes the benevolent father, who is reverenced so long as he conforms to the social mores and does not challenge or even question the parishioners' values and worldview. Direct confrontation of this worldview does not accomplish much. What is needed is conversion and a willingness to look deeper into the meaning of life. But people cannot be pushed or forced into conversion. Rather, they must be wooed or enticed through invitation and example. As a result, one important skill for pastoring in a wealthy suburb is modeling, letting people witness in the lives of the pastor, staff, and leaders what following Jesus entails; how the Scriptures are lived out in daily life; how a simple way of life that de-emphasizes material things brings joy and happiness; and how a commitment to care for one another is what really matters. All the programs or projects or creative liturgies are worthless unless people can perceive in them a depth, genuineness, and love they don't find in other areas of their lives. The emphasis is on who the pastor is rather than what he accomplishes.

Finally, in a small town or rural parish, a pastor needs special gifts to be a leader. Because there are so many rural, small town parishes in the country, they will be the first ones to experience the growing shortage of priests. The skills required of a pastor in this setting are primarily to enable people—to give them the ability, tools, and training—to take over the leadership of the parish when there is no longer a resident priest and then to empower people—

to give them the responsibility—to make decisions on their own. The pastor must also help the parishioners bridge the gaps between other Catholic parishes in the surrounding area, so that services, programs, and activities can be combined and shared. This is all done with an eye toward the day when the parish, if it is to survive, will have to do most of its ministering on its own, without a resident priest. Pastoring in a rural parish, in other words, is best done by a pastor's becoming less and less necessary and indispensible.

For pastors who wish to become more effective leaders of successful parishes, we offer the following list of do's and don'ts:

Do

1. Preside at parish liturgies in a way that makes people feel welcomed, prayerful, and challenged by God's Word.

2. Guide the parish community on its journey of faith by pointing the direction, paying attention to the inspiration of the Spirit, and leading people back to the right path when they get off track.

3. Facilitate the running of the parish, not by making all the final decisions, but by providing the opportunity for parish leaders to work together on common goals and priorities.

4. Ratify the decisions of the staff and council to give their programs and plans for the parish legitimacy and support.

5. Delegate parish responsibilities to others, leaving yourself free to be the spiritual leader of the people rather than to administrate the physical or financial needs of the parish.

6. Set the tone for renewal, spiritual growth, and shared leadership in the parish, not by direct action so much as by encouraging others to work toward these ends in the parish.

7. Provide a two-way link between the diocese and parish community, both as the representative of the bishop in the local

area and as the voice of the people to the diocese and larger Church.

8. Challenge the people to live out the Gospel, especially in areas that may not be getting enough emphasis, such as service to the poor or issues of social justice.

9. Uphold the teachings of the Church so that people are kept informed of and given guidance on moral issues.

10. Be present to the people at key moments in the life of the parish community, both joyful and painful, so that they realize you are with them in good times and bad.

Don't

1. Be the boss or sole owner of the parish. Instead, share the responsibility and burden of pastoral leadership with others.

2. Be the doer of all that needs to be done, especially if people fail to show up as promised. It is better to allow a program or activity to fail than to rush in to fill the vacuum.

3. Be the only decision maker. Let others influence and change your opinion. It may turn out to be a better decision in the long run.

4. Be laissez-faire and give up all responsibility as pastor of the parish. Being a strong leader does not mean taking over total control of the parish. Being a strong but nondomineering, pastor means accepting the role as guide and instigator of spiritual growth and renewal for the parish community, a task accomplished by working with other parish leaders for the benefit of the parish.

Putting Leadership into Practice

There are many ways to overcome the problems and reinforce the possibilities of pastoring in a modern Catholic parish. Training should begin with the young, while they are in the formative stages. In order to prepare priests for effective pastoring, the Church must train them in an environment that readies them for what is to come. Pastors often complain, ''I was never trained for this. All my theology is worthless in helping me lead meetings, deal with conflicts, and build community among staff and parish leaders.'' Not only do priests need to learn these skills early in their training, they also need to acquire them in an environment similar to a parish situation. All, or at least some, of seminary training, therefore, should be done in a collaborative context that includes mixed groups of men and women, all of whom are being trained for pastoral ministry and parish leadership.

Spiritual growth and development are essential to good pastoring. People look to their pastor to model an experience of God that speaks to their own longings. A pastor, for his own well-being as well as for his ministry, needs a lifelong pattern of prayer, retreats, spiritual direction, and support. What is needed is an established tradition of spiritual growth and development for all priests, so that the pastor is not alone in his efforts to find space and time for renewal. This spiritual emphasis should be an accepted practice, well known to the parishioners, so that all those in pastoral leadership positions are given time off for reflection, retreats, and renewal. The bishop and diocesan offices should establish and maintain this routine and tradition of spiritual growth.

Good matching is essential to good pastoring. Not all priests will be good pastors in all parishes. Different skills and abilities are required for each one. It is unfair to priests and to parishioners to match up the wrong person with the wrong parish. Much of this responsibility falls on the shoulders of the diocesan personnel board. In recent years priests have had some say about where they would like to serve as pastor. But do the people have a say about the person they want? Obviously, if priests are in short supply, the parishioners may have to settle for what they can get, but much more attention needs to be paid to the proper matching of pastor and parish. A poor match gets both parties off to a bad start, causing pain and hurt for the people, anxiety and frustration for the pastor.

Priests should be trained for the job of pastor before they are appointed. Workshops and training sessions, while helpful, are not enough. Priests need on-site experience, perhaps an internship or interim experience in a situation that includes supervision, feedback, and evaluation. This, of course, was the intention of the associate pastor position. Unfortunately, associates are often assigned to parishes in which the example of good pastoring is not present, nor is there an opportunity for feedback or consultation about what pastoring is all about. But if some parishes were identified as training centers for new pastors, priests would be given supervision and have a chance to talk over what will be required of them once they become pastors.

After he is assigned to a parish, every new pastor should be required to participate in a yearlong process of team building. Along with the staff, he should learn the skills of information gathering, decision making, community building, conflict management, and evaluation. An outside facilitator should be made available to help the pastor, staff, and parish leaders air feelings, frustrations, and hopes for the future. Other resources should also be available to the pastor and pastoral leaders whenever the need arises. One such resource might be a ''ditch companion'' for every new pastor: an experienced pastor or person skilled in group work and interpersonal communication.

Finally, every pastor should receive periodic evaluation of his pastoring abilities and skills. Just as other members of the staff are subject to contractual commitments, job descriptions, and evaluations, so should the pastor be. The evaluation could include a self-assessment, consultation, and input from staff and parishioners. Most priests do not have the benefit of such feedback, which is so necessary for personal growth, support, and affirmation. How long a pastor stays in a parish could be flexible depending on his desires and the needs of the parish. But no matter how long the tenure, periodic evaluations are essential for maintaining a successful pastorate.

Much is demanded of the pastor, who is responsible for setting the tone and direction of the parish. No amount of preparation or ongoing development is too much for all that is required of a modern pastor. However, the pastor does not have to go it alone. The marvelous reality of the modern parish is that hundreds of people are answering the call to be ministers in their parish and in their everyday lives. There is no shortage of workers. All that is needed is a pastor who can unleash these untapped resources for ministry and pastoral leadership.

NOTES

1. See Thomas Sweetser, *Successful Parishes: How They Meet the Challenge of Change* (Minneapolis: Winston Press, 1983) for a more extensive description of the various types of Catholic parishes in the United States.

Further Reading

Bausch, William J. *Traditions, Tensions, Transitions in Ministry.* Mystic, Conn.: Twenty-third Publications, 1982.

Bishops' Committee on Priestly Life and Ministry. *Human Sexuality and the Ordained Priesthood.* Washington, D.C.: National Conference of Catholic Bishops, 1983.

Lindgren, Alvin and Norman Shawchuck. *Let My People Go: Empowering Laity for Ministry.* Nashville: Abingdon Press, 1980.

Whitehead, Evelyn Eaton, and James D. Whitehead. *The Emerging Laity: Returning Leadership to the Community of Faith.* New York: Doubleday and Co., 1986.

Chapter 3

SUCCESSFUL PASTORING:
EMERGING ROLES

In the last chapter we described the problems of and the possibilities for being a pastor in a Catholic parish. But pastors are not the only ones exercising a pastoral role in the parish. In recent years the duties and responsibilities once reserved to the pastor have been assumed by others: the associate pastor, the permanent deacon, the pastoral associate, and the parish administrator. Each of these persons has a unique role with its own particular benefits and problems.

The Role of the Associate Pastor

Associate pastor is the title given to the priests in the parish who are not the pastor.[1] In the past these priests were called the assistant, or the curates. Since the Second Vatican Council, the designation has been changed to reflect a shift from a hierarchical to a more collegial model.

The new title of associate pastor may be temporary, however. This is not because it is inappropriate, but because there may not be any priests left to assume the position. Today over half of the Catholic parishes in the United States are staffed by only one priest. Some of the rural parishes must share their priest with neighboring parishes. This trend toward one-priest parishes will continue in the years ahead. Soon the presence of an associate pastor will become the exception rather than the rule.

But while the supply lasts, what role or function does the associate pastor play in the parish? The unique role of the associate pastor is sacramental. For the moment, at least, only priests can preside at the Eucharist, give absolution, and anoint the sick. In the parish the associate offers a style and tone to the celebration of the Mass and sacraments that is uniquely his own. If there is only one priest in the parish, no matter how gifted and creative he may be, his style will not suit everyone's tastes. Where there are two priests, there is a greater chance that they will differ in their approach to the Mass and sacraments, and therefore will appeal to a greater audience.

The associate role does not include the administrative concerns of the parish to the same extent as does the pastor's. Instead, the associate is freer to be more accessible to special interest groups, such as the young, singles, or newcomers. His contribution is to respond to special problems rather than to make the final decisions. Because of this, the associate is in a better position to hear what people might not tell the pastor. His job, in other words, is to share the pastoring role, but without the cares, worries, or concerns of the pastor, who is ultimately responsible for the welfare of the parish and its members.

Advantages and Difficulties

The associate pastor, in most cases, will be younger than the pastor. He is more likely to approach the liturgy with newer and more creative ideas. The associate also has the advantage of being able to specialize in various aspects of pastoral ministry, while the pastor must oversee all areas of parish life. As a result, the associate is able to spend more time with sacramental preparation, teenagers, or the catechumenate.

The associate has the luxury of being able to make mistakes during his early years as a priest and to learn from these mistakes. Parishioners are willing to give the associate room to manuever, allowing him to try out new approaches and to explore creative ideas. If he fails, it does not have the same impact or effect it would if the pastor failed. Because the pastor has final authority, the associate doesn't have to be concerned about money matters, diocesan pressures, or parish personnel. He can devote his energies to the people and to their concerns, instead.

People can relax with him, relate to him more as an equal, allow him to be human. In fact, because he is not the pastor, the associate has the great advantage of learning from the people he serves. If he is open to this benefit, he can allow the people to minister to him as well. But this presumes open and honest communication between the associate and the people. He runs the risk, because he is ordained, of parishioners placing him on a pedestal beyond the reach of criticism and evaluation. When this happens, the associate is protected, instead of challenged, by those he serves. When such a situation occurs, it not only hampers the associate's growth as a priest, but also affects his ministry in the future, especially when he assumes the role of pastor. It is while he is an associate that he must learn the art of collaboration and teamwork. It will be much more difficult to learn these lessons when he is a pastor.

Besides the danger of being set apart and protected from criticism and honest feedback, the associate is also subject to other difficulties and problems inherent in his role. For instance, because he is the associate and not the pastor, parishioners tend not to take him seriously or to accept his decisions and positions. Parishioners go over his head and appeal to the pastor for the final say. As a result, the associate may often feel like a baby priest at a time when other men his age have much more responsible positions of leadership. If the pastor does not back up the associate or give him adequate responsibility, he will feel alienated from the pastor. Because the priests usually live under the same roof, the tension between pastor and associate can become an unbearable burden, affecting at-home time, as well as on the job performance.

Another difficulty lies in the changing understanding of pastoral ministry and in the ongoing question of who is responsible for what areas of parish life and leadership. With the burgeoning new ministries in the Church today, the associate may look around and see others doing jobs he thought belonged to him. The deacon is preaching and doing the baptisms. The ministers of care are visiting the hospitals and homebound; not only do they bring Communion to the sick, they are, in effect, hearing the people's confessions as they encourage patients to tell them their concerns and worries. The youth minister takes care of the teenagers. The adult education coordinator handles the religious education programs. Others on the staff run Renew, the Rite of Christian Initiation of Adults (RCIA), and even homily preparations. The associate is there to do their bidding. What's left? Preside at Mass and keep smiling. At least the pastor has a title. What does the associate have? Whatever is left over.

This, of course, is an exaggeration, but it does describe a rising fear among associates. The fear will grow so long as the associate considers himself as being someone apart from the people and not one of many working together in a collaborative effort to bring God and God's people closer together.

All the ingredients required for the formation of a successful pastor are necessary for the successful associate as well. Formation and growth are not the sole responsibility of the associate, however. Others on the staff, parish leaders, and parishioners themselves have a responsibility to befriend the associate pastor and to let him know how much they appreciate his pastoral ministry. But they also have to speak freely to the associate about areas that need development. In other words, the people need to appreciate their associate while they still have him, but not idolize him. The associate needs honest feedback as much as the parish needs his unique gifts and fresh approaches to pastoral ministry.

As a way of challenging, as well as appreciating, the contribution of the associate pastor to parish life, we offer the following do's and don'ts:

Do

1. Work with the pastor. Give him understanding and support, but also be honest about your insights, feelings, and concerns so that there is open communication and dialogue between you. Complement the pastor's ministry by responding to people he may not be able to reach.

2. Celebrate Mass and the sacraments with all the creativity and care that you can muster, not so much as the one in charge, but as the one who helps people pray and meet their God.

3. Listen to the people as one who is available and as one who accepts human weakness, limitations, and failings. Come to know the people as friends and not as people who "receive" your priestly ministry.

4. Cooperate with other staff members, co-workers, and lay leaders, learning from their experience and unique perceptions of ministry as well as sharing your own insights. Practice working as a team member and not as a loner.

5. Respond to special needs with new approaches and creative programs, taking risks and not being afraid to learn from your mistakes.

6. Be patient and live with the givens and limitations of the situation, working for change where possible, knowing that you will only see a small part of the results of your labors before moving on to another assignment.

Don't

1. Criticize the pastor behind his back or create factions and divisions in the parish so that the pastor is the leader of one parish community, and you the leader of another.

2. Be invisible so that although you work hard in your own area of ministry, no one else on the staff or in leadership positions is aware of what you are doing.

3. Be the messiah and try to do all the work yourself, have all the answers about what is needed in the parish, or become indispensible so that when you leave, all the ministries you were responsible for collapse.

4. Take over jobs others can do, so that instead of furthering lay ministry and initiative, you stifle it. This also means being careful not to start up splinter groups in competition with existing parish organizations and programs so that parishioners are vying with one another rather than working as a united community of faith.

5. Get caught in the administrative and financial concerns of the

parish. It does help your future work as a pastor if you learn how a parish functions, but this is a time of experimentation and creativity in pastoral ministry rather than a preparation for running a business or corporation.

The Role of the Permanent Deacon

One result of Vatican II was the reinstatement of the permanent diaconate to provide a service and support to priestly ministry. The primary role of the deacon is to serve the people of God. But that's what the priests, staff, and other parish ministers are also supposed to do. What is unique about the deacon's role?

First he provides the link between parish and people, because he shares the same daily experience of work, family, and home life as the parishioners. (For the present only men are deacons. For those who are married, however, many of their wives are as much deacons as they are, and many have much more experience in parish ministry than the deacons themselves.) But as someone who has received the sacrament of Holy Orders, the deacon also shares, at least to some extent, the legitimacy and recognition given to priests.

Because of this dual experience, the deacon acts as the link between priests and people. He knows, through personal experience, the joys and pains, the difficulties and successes, facing the people he serves. He can approach them with understanding and identify with their cares. His lived experience enriches his pastoral ministry. He is also in touch with the feelings and attitudes of the people, so he is able to communicate this to the pastor and staff.

The sacramental ministry for which the deacon is responsible—preaching, performing baptisms and marriages—should be carried out with this intermediary role in mind. The deacon proclaims and preaches the Word of God out of a lived experience, speaking the people's language, not spiritual or theological platitudes. He baptizes children and adults often remembering his own children's initiation into the family of faith. He officiates at weddings, often knowing what marriage entails and how it takes a lifetime to complete what is begun in the marriage ceremony.

The permanent deacon's intermediary role is even more essential in a black, Hispanic, native American, or any predominantly ethnic parish in which the priests do not share the same cultural or racial background as the people. If the deacon shares that background, he is the only ordained minister who can uniquely understand the people's needs, desires, and expectations.

This ideal of linking priests and people is not always achieved in reality. Many deacons are older and have difficulty with newer approaches to liturgy, ministry, and post–Vatican II teachings. Despite their training, they may not be good preachers. Because of their work experience in the business world, the concept of team ministry or co-responsibility may be foreign to them. Deacons may also find this intermediary role difficult because they are in touch with a single segment of the parish and must learn how to relate to those who are of another culture, race, age, or educational background.

Advantages and Difficulties

One advantage is that the deacon has the joy of knowing he is responding to a call from the parish community and from God to be of service to others. It is an ancient call, going back to the first followers of Jesus. He keeps that tradition alive in the modern Church. With this call comes the necessity of much dedication, sacrifice, and years of preparation. It is worth the cost, however, as the deacon discovers the benefit of learning more about the Church, grows in a spiritual dedication to Jesus, and finds he has unique gifts and talents to offer parish ministry.

Another advantage of being a deacon is the privilege of serving as a model for the parish and Church. In most cases he is a married man with a family, but he is also ordained. This provides a model of a married clergy, of a dedicated parishioner, and a person who is willing to serve the Church, not for a year or two, but for as long as he is able to serve and is needed. The deacon is also given the credentials of community leader. He has the right to proclaim the Word, to gather the people together for prayer, sacraments, spiritual growth, and adult learning.

The deacon can also channel his particular unique gifts into special ministries in the parish: marriage counseling, pastoral care, prison or hospital ministry, sacramental preparation, or directing the catechumenate. The possibilities are as varied as the deacons who answer the call. The advantage of being associated with this new area of pastoring is that it is still developing and being redesigned as it grows. We have not as yet realized the full potential of deacons in American Catholic parishes.

However, we have begun to realize many of the difficulties associated with this new calling. First of all, deacons find themselves pulled in many directions, responsible for job, family, and parish ministry. Much is expected of the deacon, and the pastor, other parish leaders, and parishioners may have many unrealistic expectations. Thus, the deacon must budget his time so that he can balance his many duties and responsibilities.

Because the role of deacon is not yet well defined, he can fall into the trap of being a mini-cleric or ''little priest.'' Either his own inclinations or the expectations of others may cause the deacon to assume many of the negative aspects of clericalism and to become part of the ordained/nonordained caste system. As a result he may be looked upon with suspicion by some of the staff, lay leaders, and parishioners. Even if he is able to avoid these negative connotations, he is still considered a person set apart and therefore isolated and insulated from those who were once close. Those with whom he works or socializes may respect him but see him as ''too holy'' for future contact. He is not a priest, but he is not a ''regular'' person either.

The pressure of being set apart is often felt by the deacon's family as well. When a man is ordained deacon, it can happen that his wife and children become deacons by association; their new status is not always of their choosing. The families of Protestant ministers have had to deal with this aspect of ministry for many generations and attest to the pressures it can place on the entire family.

Another difficulty with the permanent diaconate is that it may limit, rather than enhance, the growth of lay ministry in a parish. When people know there is a deacon (or deacons) in the parish who can perform the liturgical, educational, and social ministries, they may not feel as obligated to volunteer their own time and talents. The deacon may find it difficult to get across to the people that his role is to encourage shared ministry and become the occasion for parishioners' involvement rather than to take the place of others in ministry.

The deacon can also find it difficult to break into the leadership or decision-making structure of the parish. In most cases he is a part-time member of the staff and therefore is unable to attend many staff meetings. Schedules for Masses and sacraments are given to him by the priests, jobs are assigned to him by the staff, and he may have little chance to participate in the scheduling or job assignments. He may feel like an outsider looking in on the running and operation of the parish. He may not have the level of training and expertise others on the staff have, and this also puts him at a disadvantage.

In addition, because the deacon's role and job description are still being defined, if there is a change in pastors and the new pastor does not understand or accept the work and ministry of the permanent deacon, the deacon may be left with no outlet for his dedication and commitment. Put in other words, the ministry of the deacon is often still subject to the whim of the pastor. If the diaconate fits into the pastor's vision and understanding of Church, then it will thrive in a particular parish. If not, it will fade and die for lack of support and nourishment. This risk is incurred at all levels of pastoring in the parish, not just the diaconate.

To the permanent deacon of the parish, we suggest the following do's and don'ts:

Do

1. Establish a set of priorities for yourself so that you know what comes first in your life and when to say no. Be sure you have a support structure to keep challenging you to do this.

2. Clarify your areas of responsibility and ministry in the parish for yourself and for others.

3. Act as a model of a dedicated parishioner who can answer a call to ministry and devote his life to the service of others. Continue that modeling by deepening your faith and family life, renewing your commitment to service, and learning more about current trends and emphases in the Church.

4. Form a bridge between priests and people, keeping communication open between both groups and listening to the needs of the people, especially those who are powerless. Support and work with the priests and staff in this effort of bridging gaps.

5. Encourage others to participate in the leadership and ministry of the parish. Your work is to provide new openings and opportunities for lay ministry rather than to limit or curtail its development.

6. Spread the good news, not only at Mass and in the parish, but in the work and leisure places of your life. Living out the Word has much more impact than preaching it.

Don't

1. Become isolated in your ministry so that you become a one-man show and so indispensible that the work can not continue without you.

2. Spread yourself so thin that you can't do justice to any of your many commitments and ministries or allow time for your own rest and leisure.

3. Be a mini-priest so that you take on whatever the priests have left behind. If you do, your entire ministry will become a shadowing of the priestly office and nothing will be uniquely your own. If you make yourself a mini-priest, you run the danger of forcing people to see you as one who is set apart rather than one who serves.

4. Be closed to new developments in the Church, especially those that stress shared ministry, team building, care for the poor, and social justice.

The Role of the Pastoral Associate

The pastoral associate is distinguished from the associate pastor in that the former is not ordained but performs the work of the priests with the exception of presiding at Mass and administering the sacraments.

Because the pastoral associate, in most cases, is a woman, she adds the feminine qualities to parish ministry, complementing the priests and deacons and validating the role of women in parish leadership positions.

The pastoral associate might take the place of a resident pastor in those parishes that do not have a priest living in the parish, or the pastoral associate may work as a staff or team member along with the pastor and other staff members. The staff position is even more recent than is the permanent deacon's, and its job description varies a great deal in American Catholic parishes. Some persons with the title of pastoral associate are in charge of the pastoral care in the parish. Their work is to be sure the sick and shut-ins are visited and Holy Communion brought to them.

Our definition of pastoral associate is broader. What we mean by the title is someone who shares the pastoral role in the parish, providing the same care, concern, and leadership as the pastor, but with a different perspective and emphasis. The pastoral associate plays a role similar to that of the associate pastor and deacon. She provides a link between the priests and people, offers an alternative style and approach from that of the pastor and priests, helps the staff and lay leaders work together as a team, and responds to special needs and concerns of the parishioners, especially those related to women. She also shares in the decision making and running of the parish, supports and affirms the pastor, providing him with honest and challenging feedback, enables the parishioners to assume a greater degree of ownership and leadership in the parish, and uses her unique gifts to serve the parish and Church as a whole. In effect, the pastoral associate helps to redefine the roles of ordained and nonordained ministries in the parish, showing that the boundaries between the two are not nearly as clear and distinct as they were just a few years ago.

Advantages and Difficulties

Many of the women now assuming the role of pastoral associate were once teachers in Catholic schools, primarily at the elementary level. As more and more Catholic schools closed, these women assumed the responsibility of directing religious education programs for children attending public schools. As the emphasis in religious formation shifted from the children to the parents of children in the religious education programs, the directors shifted their emphasis as well.

They returned to school to acquire skills in adult education and pastoral ministry and returned to the parish to work with adults rather than with children. This is one of the advantages, as they describe it, of working as a pastoral associate. They can be part of people's adult development, of their conversion experience, their growth in faith and religious commitment. They witness, firsthand, parishioners being transformed from marginal to active Catholics, from Mass-goers to leaders in the parish.

Pastoral associates are generally accepted in the role of pastor. Pastoral associates speak of sharing with people those times when they are most open and vulnerable: when they are sick, dying, in crisis, or undergoing transitions. People trust pastoral associates: they feel comforted; they confess their sins to them and feel they are forgiven; they can pray with them and, in a sense, celebrate liturgy together. Thus, pastoral associates are creating an environment in which people can learn about and experience God in a new way.

In other words, the advantage of being a pastoral associate is the acceptance and affirmation received from the people to whom one ministers. The pastoral associate also knows that she is breaking new ground in the Church and experiences the joy of not only being useful in the parish, but also being living proof of the many benefits women can provide to the Church.

Some of the rural parishes that do not have a resident priest but are led by a pastoral associate were hesitant at first to accept a woman in the pastoring role. But after a year or more of a pastoral associate's dedicated and sensitive concern, they became so pleased with her leadership that they wondered what it would be like if and when they had a priest assigned to them as pastor once again. Would he have the some level of empathy and understanding as the pastoral associate had? Some parishioners may not relate to the pastoral associate as well as to a priest, but others find it refreshing to have a woman in a pastoring position. This, too, is an advantage she offers to the parish: the people who come to her otherwise might not be ministered to at all.

The pastoral associate also brings fresh insights to the decision-making process of the parish. That is why the pastoral associate should be included in all the critical plans of the parish. She has the advantage of being in touch with a unique segment of the parish, especially the marginal and less articulate people. The temptation is to free her entirely of the administrative, budgeting, and financial cares of the parish. But her perspective is important, and parish planners can benefit from her suggestions and views.

But with every new position comes headaches, growing pains, and misconceptions. Because most pastoral associates are women, one disadvantage is being a woman in a male Church. It is difficult to be patient with the slow rate of change, to be left out of parish decision making, or to be criticized and scrutinized by parishioners. Too often, the pastoral associate is taken for granted, expected to do the "women's work," given extra jobs with no extra time to do them. Whenever there is a change of pastors or a cut-back in funding, she may be at the mercy of the pastor or council, for her position may be discontinued. As a woman, she is often mistrusted, suspected of ulterior motives, and subjected to sexual advances and sexist humor. She is passed over for advancement or financial rewards, not taken seriously by the people who go over her head to the "boss" when they don't like her methods or decisions, accused of being too feminine or too masculine, too passive or too aggressive. Sometimes she is treated as second-rate by the priests and as a substitute and a last resort by the people. Too often she has to settle for a low salary with few benefits and no job security, and although better trained than many of the priests, she is not allowed to minister in areas that may be best suited to her talents: preaching the Word, presiding at Eucharist, and granting absolution. Still, people answer the call, women and a few men, members of religious orders and, increasingly, laity. It may be the will of the Spirit that this area of parish leadership takes root and flourishes, despite the drawbacks and disadvantages that accompany it.

To provide some direction and perspective to people entering this field or now serving as pastoral associates, we offer the following list of do's and don'ts:

Do

1. Enter the work with the full realization that you will not be accepted by all. Have a realistic awareness of your own attitudes and limitations and your reasons for undertaking the work and insist on a clear job description.

2. Build trust among the priests, staff, lay leaders, and parishioners so that people see you as an asset and not as a threat. Be ready not only to support and affirm the priests and people, but to challenge them as well. You are breaking new ground and challenging old and lasting traditions. Be ready for the adverse reactions this will cause, but don't relinquish the dream and vision you have come to share.

3. Work *with* and not *for* people. Both enable and empower the parishioners to assume positions of leadership and shared ministry in the parish. Form pastoring groups among the people; provide them with training and direction; gather them together for support and affirmation; and let them see, by your example, that one does not have to be ordained to be a valid minister of the Gospel.

4. Stay in touch with the people, especially the marginal, the powerless, the shy, and the inarticulate. Many of these will be women who need your concern and support. Make their problems, needs, and insights an important factor in the decision making and policy setting of the parish.

5. Be visible, especially at liturgies, special parish gatherings, planning meetings, and decision-making sessions, so that people realize you are an integral part of the parish leadership.

6. Offer your unique contribution to spirituality, religious symbols, prayer, and Gospel values. Show the leaders and parishioners that there is room for both male and female understandings of Church, religion, and faith. Although the expression of one's experience may be different, it is still the same God that lies at the heart of the mystery, a God who has made us male *and* female in God's own likeness.

Don't

1. Get caught in the menial, secretarial, and housekeeping chores of the parish and its administration. If your role is pastoring, then avoid those jobs that keep you from doing this ministry. Some pastoral associates tend to do these housekeeping tasks because it's easier than getting others to do them. But that may deny some other person a ministerial role, and it reinforces misconceptions about the work of a pastoral associate.

2. Live too close to where you work. If you are too available, people will call on you for every little concern that could easily wait for your return or could be dealt with by another. The distance between home and work provides a buffer zone and can make the difference between creative ministry and burnout.

3. Take over jobs that others can or are supposed to do. Because this role is a new one, others will assume that you do whatever they don't. Often a pastoral associate ends up taking on duties that belong to the pastor, director of religious education, or lay leaders of the parish. Your role is to create the environment for others to assume their ministerial commitment. If they see you doing it, they won't.

4. Criticize the pastor in public. Try to establish rapport with him so that he will listen and accept any feedback or comments you make concerning his style of pastoring and leadership. Relate to him in such a way that he will come to accept you as a professional minister with insights and viewpoints

on parish life that are valid even if they are not always the same as his.

The Role of the Parish Administrator

The job description of the parish administrator varies widely from parish to parish. Some consider the bookkeeper or business manager the parish administrator. Others define the role in broader terms to include management, not only of the temporal concerns of the parish—budget, personnel, salaries, fund-raising, maintenance— but also of staff interaction, communication, publicity, and parish organization.

This last definition, one to which we ascribe, puts the administrator on the same professional level as the rest of the pastoral staff. The administrator's primary role is to free the pastor and staff from the temporal cares of the parish so that they have the time and energy to perform their own ministerial duties. The specific role will vary greatly with the size and location of the parish, but in general, the administrator is responsible for the following aspects of parish life and operation: finance/budget, property, personnel, office management, planning, communication, and volunteers. We will investigate each area in order to clarify the administrator's role in the parish.

Financial responsibilities include not only the day-to-day flow of income and expenses, but budgets, periodic statements and reports, payroll management, investments, and supervision of parish fund-raising, contributions, and tithing. This is not to say that the administrator is solely responsible for these financial matters. However, with the help of supporting office staff and the advice of a finance committee, the administrator can free the pastor from the burdensome and time-consuming tasks of money matters.

The administrator's role also includes closely watching the state of the parish plant, providing a regular schedule of maintenance and upkeep, planning ahead for emergencies, providing for special needs of the elderly, handicapped, and young, and arranging adequate space and suitable environments for the various ministries and programs of the parish.

In overseeing personnel, a good administrator, with the help of the pastor and staff, makes up a personnel booklet for all the employees of the parish. This booklet should include job descriptions for paid positions, salary scales and benefits, and interviewing, hiring, and evaluation procedures. The administrator works closely with the pastor and the appropriate committee in recruiting, screening, hiring, training, and, when necessary, terminating personnel.

The administrator also supervises all support staff—secretaries, janitors, cooks, receptionists—to make certain they not only perform their tasks well, but also feel good about working in the parish. This part of the role demands good listening and conflict management skills. Office management also includes maintaining office machinery, such as typewriters, copiers, computers, and postage machines, all of which must be kept in good working order for the smooth running of the parish.

The administrator also participates in parish planning, not only for the physical growth and development of the parish, but for the spiritual needs of the people as well. The administrator, along with a planning committee, acts as a resource person, providing the expertise and skills for effective parish planning. This is not to reduce the parish to the level of a well-managed business. Rather, the administrator plays a key role in helping the pastor, staff, and council establish parish priorities, set new directions, and make plans for the future, so that the limited resources of the parish can be used to best advantage.

Good communication is also within the sphere of the administrator's role. This means keeping open the lines of communication between leaders and people. The administrator oversees the flow of information to parishioners, including the bulletin, newsletter, special mailings, letters, and notices. The administrator ensures that census information is updated and is stored in an easily accessible manner, that parishioners have the opportunity to give feedback on parish procedures and decisions, and that groups and individuals with special needs and concerns are heard.

Much of the time and energy of an administrator is taken up with volunteers, that is, parishioners who have given of their time and talent to help out in the parish. The administrator makes sure that volunteers know what is required of them, that they are adequately trained, that they are held responsible for completing tasks, and that they experience satisfaction, recognition, and support for their work.

Advantages and Difficulties

Most parish administrators are surprised to find themselves in this ministry. Some have come from managerial occupations; others have discovered, while working as volunteers in the parish, that they have a gift for organization and management. The first advantage they discover in their new work is that they can use their skills and past experience to benefit the parish and to further God's work.

They discover that they are being challenged by the many and varied demands of their work and find they can, in most cases, rise to meet crises with energy and enthusiasm. Many administrators mention the freedom and flexibility they enjoy in managing the parish. They speak highly of the authority and support the pastor gives them to make the decisions necessary to their work and sphere of influence. Such a climate is often very different from that which they have experienced in previous jobs.

Administrators are also happy to be able to work in a loving and caring environment with others who are dedicated to parish ministry, in a manner that frees others to be better pastoral ministers. In this way, even the most trivial task can contribute to the life of the parish. The parish administrator's side benefits, ones never mentioned in the contract, are also most appealing. These include the support and friendship of other staff members, the affirmation and appreciation of volunteers and parish ministers, the acceptance and praise of pastor and people. Administrators become aware that because they are helping the parish run smoothly, the parishioners are enjoying the parish more and finding more of their needs being met.

But there are drawbacks to the job as well. For instance, it is difficult to keep people happy, especially when they come to the administrator all at once, each one asking for help, materials, repairs, or more money. Although the administrator would like to please everyone, the parish must still operate within financial and physical limits. In the midst of such demands, it is difficult to keep parish priorities in mind, that is, to remember that the budget is to be of service to the needs of the people and parish ministries, and not the reverse.

The administrator must often cope with conflicting demands from staff, leaders, and people and must make difficult decisions. In some parishes the pastor gives over all authority for temporal affairs to the administrator and doesn't provide enough support when hard decisions must be made. In other parishes the pastor does not let go of the controls, so that the administrator cannot make any decision without the pastor's approval. Both extremes cause anxiety for the administrator. The administrator is also in the same precarious situation as the pastoral associate: poor job security. If a new pastor assigned to the parish does not feel the need for an administrator, it isn't long before the position is no longer required in the parish.

Finally, the danger of becoming overextended and burned out is very real for an administrator. The temptation is to look on the work not only as a job or even a ministry, but as a personal possession, one that stays with the person day and night. The parish "belongs" to the administrator. Any crisis or conflict that comes up becomes his or her personal affair. The distance between one's own life and the ministry is lost. No one can survive long in such a situation. When the administrator is too close to his or her work, the parish also suffers. The situation keeps people from becoming involved in the parish: parishioners believe that someone will always be there to fix the pipes, restack the chairs, set up the room, or make the coffee.

To reinforce the advantages and overcome the difficulties, we offer the following advice to the parish administrator:

Do

1. Be a person of faith so that the work of administrating the parish is not a job so much as a ministry. This means keeping a proper balance between the physical or temporal needs of the parish and the spiritual needs of the people.

2. Free others, especially the pastor, so that they can perform their works of mercy, pastoral care, education, worship, and spiritual leadership in the parish. Keep the pastor informed, but do not bother him with unnecessary details.

3. Be competent in the management of the parish. The staff and lay leaders will look upon you with confidence, knowing you can take care of emergencies when they arise with the least amount of disruption to the life of the parish.

4. Plan the budget and finances of the parish in a manner that reflects Christian values and Gospel imperatives. Convey to the parishioners that their contributions are used to help build the parish community and aid the needy.

5. Keep open the communication lines between the staff and parish workers, between parish groups, and between members of the parish. Keep in touch with shifting membership and changing neighborhood patterns and allow them to be reflected in parish priorities.

6. Work behind the scenes so that those who are more visible are given the tools, information, and support to be effective leaders in the parish.

Don't

1. Be a glorified bookkeeper, secretary, or janitor in the parish, so that you end up doing all the menial chores and have no time left over to manage the parish. Insist on being given the amount of authority commensurate with your role in the parish.

2. Be the pastor or controller of the parish, so that people look on you as stingy with parish funds. For the sake of efficiency and good management, don't become a "dictator" in the parish.

3. Spread yourself too thin. The temptation is to take on too much. Manage the important areas of parish management but delegate the details and the implementation of policies to other employees and volunteers. Doing so does them a service; it

lets them use their gifts for the parish, and it frees you for the tasks you were hired to perform.

4. Be always available so that people know how to find you any time or any place when minor needs arise. If they can't always find you, they will learn to use their own initiative and creativity in discovering solutions. It allows them to feel useful and worthwhile. Better to create vacuums so that people can fill them with their own dedication and commitment rather than to fill up the vacuums yourself before others know that a problem exists.

5. Run the parish like IBM or General Motors. It is one thing to keep the parish running smoothly; it is another to have it be so efficient that people feel they belong to a business or corporation rather than to a faith community.

Along with many other participants, these four persons—associate pastor, deacon, pastoral associate and parish administrator—make up a modern parish staff. The way that this staff works together is crucial to creating a successful parish.

NOTES

1. The 1983 Code of Canon Law refers to the associate pastor as the *assistant priest* (Canons 541–552). (See the Canon Law Society of Great Britain and Ireland, *The Code of Canon Law in English Tradition* [London: Collins, 1983], p. 98-100.) We use the more common term *associate pastor* because it connotes a more equal, collaborative relationship between the priests serving in the parish.

Further Reading

Campbell, Thomas C., and Gary Reierson. *The Gift of Administration*. Philadelphia: Westminster Press, 1981.

Fuller, Robert D. *Adventures of a Collegial Parish*. Mystic, Conn.: Twenty-third Publications, 1981.

Gilmour, Peter. *The Emerging Pastor*. Kansas City, Mo.: Sheed and Ward, 1986.

O'Brien, J. Stephen, ed. *Gathering God's People: Signs of a Successful*

Parish. Huntington, Ind.: National Catholic Education Association with Our Sunday Visitor, Inc., 1982.

Weidman, Judith L., ed. *Women Ministers: How Women are Redefining Traditional Roles*. San Francisco: Harper & Row, 1981.

Chapter 4

PARISH STAFF: BOTH MODEL AND RESOURCE

In evaluating the role of the parish staff, several questions must be answered. Who makes up the staff? What function do staff members play in the parish? How do they interact with one another?

The Definition of Staff

Before Vatican II it was easy to decide who made up the staff. The parish staff consisted of the pastor and his assistant priests. Today, given the growing complexity of parish life, it isn't so easy to say who is a member of the parish staff and who is not.

Consider a fictitious parish, St. Joseph's. Suppose the pastor calls a staff meeting for Monday morning. Who should come? There are eleven staff people altogether, but only six are full-time. The two parish secretaries don't feel the staff meeting is for them, because they are not involved in pastoral planning and decision making. Their role is to complete all the detailed work, such as typing, mailings, and answering the phone. The part-time parish bookkeeper feels the same about staff meetings. All three, however, want to be kept informed about what is decided at staff meetings because it affects their work.

Therefore, we will exclude the office workers from the definition of staff. Nevertheless, these people need to feel that they are part of the pastoral care of the parish community. They receive the phone calls, answer the door bell, and forward requests to the appropriate pastoral minister. As a means of including the office workers, the staff of St. Joseph's has one Monday morning meeting every month that involves the extended staff, pastoral ministers and office workers alike. At this meeting staff members clear up difficulties and communicate their concerns. In between these monthly meetings, it is the pastor's task to meet with the office workers to keep them up-to-date on recent changes in policy and parish developments, so they will know what is happening when parishioners call.

Once the office workers have been dropped from the definition of parish staff, eight people remain: four full-time, two part-time, and two permanent deacons who volunteer their time. The Monday morning staff meeting, which is fine for the full-time staff, may be difficult for the two part-time people to attend and leaves the deacons out entirely. Both deacons have other jobs. Thus, they can attend only evening or weekend staff meetings. Are deacons members of the parish staff? Yes and no; much depends on their pastoral responsibilities. If they are in charge of a parish ministry—for example, the parish visiting program or family counseling—then they are members of the staff. They do not have to be at all staff meetings, only those that affect their areas of responsibility.

In order to accommodate the deacons, one staff meeting a month is held in the evening. These evening meetings keep the deacons informed about parish events, plan and give feedback about the ministries they direct. The deacons, in effect, are adjutant, or support, staff members, but they are not members of the core pastoral staff.

The two part-time staff members, the youth minister and the music director, both have other jobs, and their involvement in the parish is limited to about twenty hours per week. Are these people really staff members? They are not interested in the overall pastoral planning of the parish to the same degree as are the other four staff members. The part-time staff members decide to opt out of all but one Monday morning meeting a month, the same one attended by the office workers. They consider themselves associate staff members.

This leaves four people, the two priests, the director of religious education, and the school principal. They make up the core pastoral staff of the parish. They are the full-time, professional staff for the pastoral ministry of the parish. They meet every Monday morning. Their meeting includes twenty minutes of prayer, twenty minutes of feedback concerning one another's ministries, and an hour and a half of planning and group decision making. Eleven people are on the general staff, which includes all aspects of the parish; but of this number, three are clerical staff (office workers), two are adjutant staff (deacons), two are associate staff (part-time members), and four are the core pastoral staff (full-time members).

The Role of the Pastoral Staff

Although the office staff is not included as part of the pastoral staff, the pastoral tone of the front office is critical because office staff is generally the first to receive a call for help from a person in critical need of financial or emotional assistance. Thus, the office staff needs training on how to deal with requests and who to contact in an emergency. But their role is not as encompassing as that of the pastoral staff of the parish.

Part of the role of the pastoral staff is to set an example and provide a model of Christian community. But these people are also the resource persons and facilitators for various parish ministries that help parishioners discover and exercise their own gifts for pastoral ministry. Both aspects are necessary for a successful staff. In light of this dual approach to parish organization, the role of the pastoral staff in the parish is clarified in the following list of do's and don'ts:

Do

1. Act as resources to specialized areas of parish ministry. The director of religious education, for instance, must be in touch with current directions and emphases in religious education in order to provide programs and texts for the education of youth and adults in the parish.

2. Enable and empower the parishioners to fulfill their responsibilities as Christian leaders and co-ministers of the Gospels. The two words *enable* and *empower* do not mean the same thing. It does no good to give a person the power to be a leader if you have not given the person training that makes

him or her able to be a leader. The staff person trains people how to be ministers and then shares the power to carry out the ministry of education or music or pastoral care.

3. Carry out the policies of the parish in specific areas. It is the task of the parish council, in conjunction with the pastor, to set overall policies. But it is the task of the staff to see that these policies are implemented in the many different areas of the parish.

4. Shake up the complacent groups of the parish, those who have settled back and stopped growing in the faith or stopped developing their full potential as leaders or pastoral ministers.

5. Keep in touch with the needs of the people, especially those people who are forgotten or who are unable to speak for themselves. This especially includes the poor, the sick and elderly, the lonely or alienated, and the shy and inarticulate parishioners.

6. Provide an example of collaborative ministry and Christian community. Parishioners should see the staff playing, planning, working, and enjoying their ministry together. Such an example of Christian living provides a model for other parish groups to follow.

Don't

1. Work independently of one another or of the parish council and parish leaders. Sometimes staff members get so involved in their own area of ministry that they forget they represent only one segment of parish life.

2. Think of yourselves as permanent parish workers. A staff member's tenure in the parish is limited. Parishioners will remain long after staff members have moved on to another

parish or area of ministry. If staff members think of themselves as temporary, they will be more likely to enable and empower the parishioners to continue the work they have begun.

3. Act as if you can do it all. Sometimes staff members think that no one can do it as well or as competently as they can. This attitude does the parish community a disservice. Staff members need to work themselves out of jobs rather than make themselves indispensable.

This last don't for parish staff refers to what we call the *theology of relinquishment:* letting go of the reins so that others can assume responsibility and initiative in ministry. People will rush in to fill vacuums if they see that no one on staff steps in to rescue a failing program or faltering project. Only through relinquishment will parishioners realize that the parish belongs to them and not to the pastor or staff.

Personalities play a part in determining staff roles and job descriptions. One person might be better at creating new programs, while another relates to people better. We can identify at least four different types of leaders: the dreamer, the goal setter, the action taker, and the harmonizer.[1] One person might have the characteristics of all four types, and that person may or may not be a pastor, associate pastor, or staff member. But whoever the persons may be, every successful parish staff should have among its members these four types.

The dreamer articulates the parish vision or dream, challenging other leaders to think creatively and to let loose the powers of possibility and "what if's." The dreamer is intuitive, creative, poetic, expansive, exciting, and future oriented. Every staff needs its Don Quixote, the maker of the "impossible dream," the person who pushes the limits of present programs and projects and keeps thinking up new ideas for liturgy, community gatherings, education, or outreach. Without this type of leader, the parish remains staid, settled, self-satisfied, and narrow.

But too much dreaming remains just that, a dream or fantasy.

Following on the heels of the dreamer comes the goal setter: the person who can translate the dream into realizable goals and priorities. This leader is able to see possibilities in what others would consider mere fantasy. This leader can establish a timetable for the dream, reduce it to bite-size portions, and give direction to others on how to achieve the dream step-by-step.

The goal setter, however, is usually not the person who gets the goals accomplished. That is up to the action taker. The action taker is pragmatic, impatient with dreams and possibilities. Once goals have been set, this leader can gather people together to get the project done. He or she is the nuts-and-bolts person who is on the scene with paper, pencils, glue, and scissors and who sees to it that what the dreamer suggested and the goal setter outlined becomes reality.

One other type of leader is essential to this process: the harmonizer. The harmonizer is a caring, sensitive person aware of the emotional climate of the group, able to soothe tempers, give moral support, and keep the other three types of leaders feeling good about themselves and communicating with one another.

Every parish staff, as well as any other group within the parish, benefits from all four types of leaders. When a staff lacks any of the four leader types, either its vision is too narrow, its goals and directions too hazy, its plans poorly implemented, or the interaction between people halting and tension laden. All four types need each other in order to create a well-functioning, successful parish staff.

Interaction Between Staff Members

A common tool for analyzing group interaction is the people-task grid shown in Figure 1. Staff interaction is plotted on two axes on this grid: the degree of commitment to people and to tasks. At the lower left corner, the county fair exemplifies unstructured interaction. People come and go and try to keep out of each other's way, but they do not relate or share in one another's affairs. This is the crowd model of staff organization: "I do my work, you do yours, and let's give each other a lot of room." This do-it-yourself style of interaction is typical of people at a county fair, on a bus, or at a sports event. The type of leadership needed in the crowd model is that provided by a traffic cop: someone who can maintain order, keep the traffic moving, and solve disputes when people get in each other's way.

At a higher level of organization on the task axis is the factory model, in which the staff is committed to getting a task accomplished. Everything else is of little importance. If people get to know one another in the process, that is good, but not significant. The atmosphere is like an assembly line in a factory: there is time for breaks and recreation, but the primary focus is on meeting production quotas. With this style of staff interaction the type of leadership needed is that of a supervisor, someone who is good at overseeing the assembly line and organizing people to accomplish the task. Because interaction focuses on the end product rather than the quality of interaction, the style of leadership is usually more authoritarian and hierarchical.

The opposite extreme of the factory model of interaction may be found in the staff that could care less about getting the job done. Staff members are much more concerned about how they relate with each other. The staff spends much time socializing, supporting one another, and sharing. Such a staff can be represented on the grid at

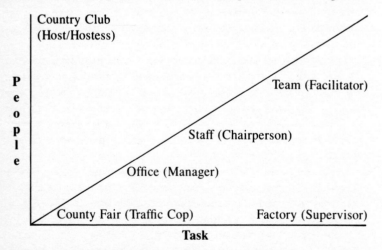

Figure 1. The People-Task Grid

Adapted from Robert Blake and Jane Srygley Mouton, *The Managerial GRID*® (Houston: Gulf Publishing Co., 1978), 11; reprinted by permission.

a higher level on the people axis: the country club style of interaction. The type of leadership needed for this style of interaction is that of host or hostess, someone who can make everyone feel at ease, get them sharing on a personal level, and help the group grow closer together. For such a staff accomplishing a task is only secondary. What is really important is the level of friendliness and openness between members of the staff.

Not many parish staffs are at either extreme of the people-task grid, although for short periods one or the other priority may predominate. When we explained this grid to a staff we once worked with, the pastor remarked that the task axis was not long enough. His style of interaction was off the page. The rest of the staff had little trouble agreeing with him.

The level of interaction can typically be plotted in the middle of the grid, with equal emphasis given to the task and to people. But the degree of the staff's commitment, both to the task or ministry and to each other, varies. At the level of commitment typical of an office, staff members are conscientious about getting jobs done and do spend time getting to know one another, but their level of commitment is limited. When on the job, the staff members accomplish their tasks and enjoy spending time with each other. But when quitting time comes, they are nowhere to be found. No demands can be made on their time away from the office.

The type of staff leadership needed in this style of interaction is that of a manager, someone who is good at parceling out tasks so that everyone's time is well used. A good manager also maintains a pleasant working environment so that people enjoy the work space and have a chance to share with each other, at least on a minimal level. However, little is expected by way of personal sharing or collaboration in ministry.

At a higher level of commitment on the diagonal line between the task and people axes is the *staff* level of interaction. In this case staff members consider their work more as a ministry than as a task to be accomplished. At the same time they are concerned about sharing in the ministry as a group and not as a collection of individuals. They devote time to their own interaction as well as to planning and evaluating as a group what is required of each one in the ministry.

At this level staff members can make demands on one another above and beyond what is strictly required of each person, and attention is given to the modeling the staff does in the parish as well as to the work individuals accomplish. The leadership needed in this form of interaction is that of chairperson, someone who can coordinate group and individual talents and gifts so that everyone feels part of the group and feels that he or she is being given enough attention, support, and freedom of movement. At the same time the group as a whole has a sense of direction, a satisfaction with its interaction, and a feeling of success in the ministry. In most staffs the pastor is the chairperson, but in some cases the leadership role may shift to another, depending on the task to be accomplished or the type of personal interaction desired.

At the highest level of commitment is the team approach to staff interaction. This is a rare occurrence in Catholic parishes. What distinguishes *team* from *staff* is the level of commitment members have made to each other and the depth of sharing that goes on with regard to staff member's particular areas of ministry. In *Successful Parishes* Thomas Sweetser defined *team* as a ministry in which ''all members of the parish staff, including the priests, share equally the leadership role of the parish. Each person on the staff has an area of competence and responsibility, but no one person is considered the head of the parish staff. All have equal voice in the important decisions of the team and of the parish.''[2]

This is an ideal to work towards, but one that is rarely achieved. People involved in teams soon realize that many difficulties are inherent in this style of interaction. In a random sample survey of seventy parish teams across the country conducted by Carol Wisniewski Holden, the following problems and difficulties were uncovered:

- Team members don't always know who is doing what.
- It takes more time to get a job done and involves more meetings.
- Mutual accountability demands more honesty.
- Interpersonal communication skills are needed by all involved.
- Communication lines break down because more people need to be informed.
- Conflicts arise when people work in overlapping areas of ministry.

- When everyone is responsible, no one takes ownership, and jobs don't get done.
- People have little past experience to draw upon and therefore don't know what to expect.[3]

If it is so difficult to interact as a team, why would a staff even attempt it? For two reasons; first, to act as a model of Christian community for other parish groups to emulate; and second, to share the roles and duties of pastoral ministry as a group rather than allowing each person to work alone in his or her own area of responsibility. The team spends time together, not just to accomplish tasks, but to share periods of prayer, to talk about what parish ministry means to them, and to tell stories about their journeys of faith, providing a model for others. In their ministry team members work together in planning projects, leading groups, and evaluating programs. If a Lenten program has to be planned, the team works with the liturgy planners brainstorming ideas, selecting the best option, and putting it into operation. If a special feast day or anniversary liturgy is coming up, it's not left to the priest or liturgy director to plan. It's a cooperative effort of the entire team.

The type of leader required for team ministry is that of a facilitator—someone who allows team members to function as equals, encourages mutual support and growth, manages conflicts between team members, and helps the group maintain a balance between getting the work done and spending time together for group and individual sharing. The role of facilitating leader may rotate so that no one person is the leader for an indefinite period, but the team does need a leader. Otherwise, as a leaderless group, it can lose its sense of purpose and fail both in providing a model of community to the parish and in getting the ministerial tasks accomplished.

Figure 2 focuses on the staff-team, people-task section of the original grid in Figure 1. The parish staff and its individual members move up and down, back and forth, along the diagramed lines. The interplay between group interaction and ministry, for instance, lies on a continuum, with some members wanting to emphasize the work that needs to be done in the parish, while others hunger for more time to get to know one another. This fluidity between staff or team and people or task makes staffing very complex and, at

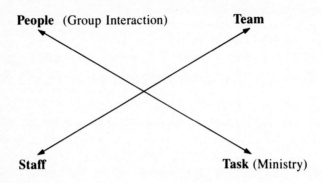

Figure 2.   The Group Interaction Continuum

times, difficult in a modern parish. (Chapter 5 discusses in detail parish staff team building.)

Collaboration between Men and Women

We begin with a case study on collaboration. This case study examines a staff in a parish situated on the edge of a changing section of the city. The parish is still predominantly white, and the average age of the parishioners is increasing. The staff consists of a pastor in his fifties, an associate pastor fresh from the seminary, an elderly nun who serves as principal of the school, a director of religious education who is a laywoman in her late thirties, and a permanent deacon in his middle fifties. The deacon's wife usually sits in on the staff meetings and is active in the pastoral care program of the parish.

Case Study:

Last month the pastor received a letter indicating that because of a cutback in funds, the city no longer will be able to rent the parish school annex for a continuing education program. This rent money had enabled the parish to maintain the school without going into debt. The pastor panicked. He called in his financial advisors and asked them what to do. They decided that closing the school was out of the question and suggested that other items could be cut back to make up for the loss. The obvious place to cut back would be the religious education budget. Perhaps the program could get along without a secretary and maybe even without a staff person. After all, the present staff person's salary was twice that of any other person on the staff. The pastor protested, but he saw the logic in his advisors' reasoning.

The pastor went to the next staff meeting with a heavy heart. Perhaps if he brought it up during the prayer, as a petition, it would not cause so much of a problem. So during the petitions, he prayed, ''That we will come together in this time of crisis when the school annex will no longer be rented by the city, let us pray to the Lord.''

The news fell like a ton of bricks. No other petitions followed. Everyone remained silent and looked at one another with confusion. This was the first hint they had of any difficulty.

After the prayer the director of religious education asked, as gently as she could, ''Joe, when did you hear this news?''

''Last week. I thought that because it was a financial matter it concerned my financial advisors more than the staff. We should spend our time here on spiritual concerns, not temporal ones.''

The director replied, ''But we are in this together, Joe, and we want to help each other out in critical times. We want to work as a team and not as separate individuals.'' She said this in an even tone, trying to control the anger and confusion she felt because the pastor was reverting to being ''in charge'' rather than confiding in the staff.

The principal, worried about her school, spoke up. ''Father, does this mean that we will have to close the school?''

''No, no, Sister,'' the pastor replied. ''We have worked it out so that nothing in the school budget will be touched. All the men supported the school and the good it is doing for the parish.''

Then, the director of religious education spoke up, ''Joe, let's get this straight. The school budget stays. But what about the religious education budget? Is that what goes?''

''Ah, yes, now that you mention it, the men advised me that perhaps we could cut back on some of the services we offer in religious education. Well, not services exactly, but perhaps some of the support structures, such as the religious education secretary. We could make up for the loss with volunteers.''

The climate of the meeting changed. The director's face got red. The young associate, who was about to jump to the director's defense, held back. He knew he had to stay on the good side of the pastor, so he kept his mouth shut. The principal, somewhat embarrassed because the school was secure but the religious education was not, wanted to support the director but did not know how, so she withdrew from the conflict.

The deacon, who had been a trustee of the parish, understood the difficulties the pastor faced in trying to pay the bills. He started to come to the defense of the pastor, but one look from his wife made him think twice about speaking up, so he remained quiet. The deacon's wife gave supportive looks to the director, but since she was not really a staff person, she kept out of the fray. The pastor, looking somewhat sheepish, suggested that they take some time to think about this matter. He then went on to the next agenda item, the communal penance service coming up next month.

Somehow everyone got through the meeting in one piece. The atmosphere remained tense over the next week. A number of one-to-one conversations took place between staff members, mostly in support of either the pastor or the director of religious education, who finally decided to make an appointment with the pastor to "get the facts."

As the meeting started, she said, "Joe, you realize that I could rally support for my programs by stirring up the religious education teachers and parents, as well as the adults in our discussion series. But this is no way to settle this issue. I joined this staff because I thought we could develop into a team ministry. But now you have reversed our direction and have gone back to making the decisions alone and announcing them to the rest of us on staff. I am not sure I can continue working in this situation. Perhaps you would like me to resign. It would take you off the hook."

The pastor replied, "Karen, you have done a great job here and have helped all of us grow together as a staff. As you know, it has been difficult for me, but I'm learning. But what am I supposed to do? I can't let this place go bankrupt."

The meeting was not a pleasant one for either the pastor or the director. At its conclusion the director suggested that someone from outside the situation be asked to help facilitate the next staff meeting, someone not as emotionally involved in the issue. This was a new approach for the pastor, but in a moment of desperation, he agreed.

At this juncture the case study has not reached a resolution, but despite the hurt on both sides, good collaboration is beginning. The individuals involved are facing up to their problem and seeking help. Unfortunately, this case study is not a unique situation. It happens in one form or another, again and again, in parishes throughout the country. The women on staff are becoming frustrated and angry with men, while the men, especially the priests, are becoming exasperated and confused. What can be done to ease the tension?

The first step toward a solution is to be aware of why the problem exists. Much depends on staff members' differing perceptions of collaboration. The differences are most pronounced between clergy— priests and deacons—and women, both religious and lay. Confusion and misunderstanding are most pronounced in five areas: personal sharing, accountability, performance, definition of team, and sexual attraction.[4]

Personal Sharing

In working with parish staffs, we have discovered that when asked to share inner feelings, women members are more at ease and comfortable than are men. Men, especially priests, find such sharing difficult and wonder what it has to do with improving staff collaboration. It is not that women spend more time talking. Men talk just as much as women. The women, however, tend to be better listeners. It is not uncommon for one of the priests to interrupt a woman staff member when she is talking because he feels the need to add something to the conversation. It is rare for a woman to interrupt one of the priests when he is talking. She will usually wait until he has finished and then add her comment.

This appears to be a small issue, but it is representative of the differences in personal and group sharing. The clergy can share ideas and insights and expect to be listened to, but they have more difficulty sharing their personal feelings, hurts, and joys. Women, on the other hand, have an easier time sharing their inner life but get frustrated when they are cut off, interrupted, or not listened to by the men on the staff. The women feel as though their contributions are not given equal value. Such experiences are not conducive to a collaborative environment.

Accountability

The degree of accountability and supervision is not the same for men—especially clergy—and for women on parish staffs. The men have more control over their use of time, both when they are on duty and when they are away from their work. No credentials other than ordination are required when clergy join the staff, and rarely will anyone question or call them to task for not being present or failing to do a job.

Others on the staff, especially women, are hired after supplying the required credentials and undergoing interviews. They have defined work hours, a detailed job description, and are held accountable if they don't get their tasks accomplished. Unlike many priests, they are subject to periodic evaluations.

The different level of accountability for men and for women is also revealed in the unequal requirement for professional education. The priests are encouraged to attend study days and seminars, but most consider themselves too busy to attend. Conversely, the women, and to a lesser extent the lay men on staff, are required to attend these events and in most cases do. As a result, the women are often more in tune with current trends and directions in the Church than are the priests. This is perceived by many priests as a threat to their intelligence and ability, which makes collaborative ministry difficult.

Obstacles to collaboration are also apparent when dealing with the roles of women and men, especially priests, on staff. Most of the men have built-in job security as priests. They are assured of a position, especially as the pool of available clergy shrinks. Once they fulfill their administrative and liturgical duties, they are free to operate on their own. The women staff members do not have this freedom or security. They usually feel the need to justify their positions on staff by becoming active in a number of parish ministries. They also realize that their jobs are dependent not only on their ability, but also on the available funds in the parish and on the approval of the pastor, the council, or the parish boards. Thus, women are more likely to document how they spend their time on the job than are men, just in case someone should ask about how they spend their day. It does not occur to most of the clergy to do this. Even age plays a part. One youth director told us, "The pastor feels that anyone working with youth should be under thirty, and I'm twenty-nine now. I wonder what next year will bring?"

This difference in roles carries over into personal behavior. The priests are provided with many helps and support structures to free them for their ministry. Someone usually washes their clothes, cleans their room, makes their bed, cooks their meals, and washes their dishes. Not so for the women on staff. After putting in a full day, and often a long evening as well, they must fend for themselves, even caring for a family besides. Staff meetings reveal this inequality. The women often provide coffee and refreshments, while the men accept the services provided by the women with much appreciation but little thought of doing the same for the women.

Many staffs now have a more equal sharing of the menial tasks associated with meetings and staff outings, but we still encounter staffs in which the priests get up from a staff meal and go into the living room to chat while the women are left to clear off the dishes and clean up. Once again, this may not be a great matter, but it is symptomatic of how difficult collaboration is when role expectations vary between men and women on staffs.

Role and power are closely related. Presently, the clergy occupy the dominant Church positions and therefore hold the power. If a woman on the staff tries to challenge this power, she is looked upon as aggressive and domineering. If, on the other hand, a priest misuses his authority by pulling rank or staging a power play, he is often viewed by the people as working within his rights and acting according to what is expected of him. Such situations destroy collaborative efforts.

The sense of powerlessness experienced by those not ordained, especially women, is most keenly felt when an important decision affecting their area of ministry is made and they are not part of the decision-making process. The case study that began this section describes one such situation. The pastor thought he was acting collaboratively. After all, he did bring the matter to his financial advisors. He also thought he was being open with the staff by bringing the issue to the staff meeting. But the decision was made before he came to the meeting. He had the power and he used it, although in a somewhat indirect and manipulative fashion. He made the decision, but the matter was not settled. The disruption of staff interaction continued until it was necessary to call in an outside facilitator to help put the pieces back together again.

We have also encountered some women staff members who have become bitter toward men because of Church structures, work situations, or family backgrounds. This resulted in misplaced anger that they expressed by misusing their positions to gain power and control. Instead of learning from past experiences and working toward reconciliation, they sought out a staff position as a way of gaining influence and establishing control over men, especially over the ordained clergy.

Collaboration is difficult in the midst of such power struggles, sometimes even impossible. Only when the use of power is changed to mutual sharing of authority and decision making does collaborative ministry grow and flourish. If the Spirit is present in our parishes today, it is acting through these efforts at collaboration. Much is working against collaborative ministry, but with God's help it is alive and, in many places, growing.

Performance

Generally, the priests are given the benefit of the doubt in the performance of their duties, especially those duties connected with the Mass and the sacraments. If their sermons are dull, they hear few complaints. If the pastor's appearance is sloppy, it is attributed to his working too hard. If the associate pastor is sharp with the altar servers, he is only keeping them in line. If the visiting priest gives a fire-and-brimstone sermon, the people accept the tirade as his way of shaking up the lax and wayward. But if one of the women staff members talks at the weekend Masses about religious education, parish renewal, or pastoral care, her attire is scrutinized and her voice criticized as too weak or too masculine or too assertive. If she tries to challenge the people or speak with authority, the people question what right she has to tell them what to do.

The two of us speak at the weekend Masses in the parishes where we conduct the Parish Evaluation Project. In subtle ways Carol has to prove herself more than does Tom. Only "Father Sweetser" is introduced as the speaker. The people are amazed that Carol can remember all the statistics from the parish survey. In leaving the church, people say goodbye to "the priest" but not to the woman standing beside him. Even when men and women work well together as a collaborative team, as we feel we do, many parishioners cannot accept them as equals.

The Definition of Team

Many parish staffs would like to work as a team, but this ideal eludes them. Why? Most often it is because the men, especially the priests, have a different concept of team ministry than do the women. Women most often think of team as a mutual sharing of ministry, as a chance to participate in the decision making, as a group of people growing closer together through prayer, shared faith, and common experiences. Their description of team might be, "We're in this together, as equals, or at least, as accepting and respectful of each other. We are willing to commit ourselves to each other and to work together on parish projects and ministries. We care for and are important to one another." The women may have other personal commitments, such as a religious community or family, but while working as part of the team, they commit themselves not only to their ministries, but also to the building up of a spirit of community and mutuality among the members of the team.

Men, on the other hand, might define team in sports-related terms. Their description might be, "Teams are great. They work together for the good of the whole. There is nothing like team work. but every team needs a coach or captain or quarterback to call the plays. That is why we have a pastor. He is in charge and we work with him to succeed." The different connotations of team for men and for women may not be so obvious, but many priests, especially pastors, wonder how a team could operate without a person in charge. They are afraid of losing control, of letting go and allowing the team to assume responsibility for itself.

One pastor told us that he was finally able to let go and not feel he was ultimately responsible when he no longer felt he was the one to tell a staff person who was late for a meeting to come on time or to inform others who were absent what went on at the meeting. Instead, he was able to challenge the entire team to be responsible to one another. It took a great load off his shoulders. Unfortunately, such a pastor, one who trusts in the staff enough to let go of the controls, is still a rare and endangered species in the American Catholic Church.

Sexual Attraction

Both the American culture and the hierarchical structure of the Church make it difficult for men and women to work together as equals in a mutually affirming, supporting environment. Our culture reinforces the dominant, controlling role of men and the submissive, seductive, mothering role of women. Add to this cultural emphasis the protective and isolating manner of priestly and religious training, and it is not surprising that men and women have difficulty relating to each other on parish staffs. But in recent years psychology has suggested that male-female interaction and friendships are important ingredients in a person's stages of personal growth.

Conflict between this need and cultural stereotypes makes staff members feel pulled in several directions at once. For example, a priest may consider a woman on the staff attractive and appealing. But at the same time, he is afraid and uncertain about his own needs for affection and sexual expression. A woman staff member, on the other hand, feels sorry for one of the priests and wants to protect him and help him become a better person. But she ends up mothering him and making him feel dependent on her.

Many priests feel threatened by the offer of affection and friendship from women staff members. They may react to this offer by losing themselves in their tasks and avoiding any level of personal sharing with women on the staff. They may withdraw completely and keep their social lives at a distance and off-limits to staff interaction. It is a safer and less threatening resolution to sexual attraction. It is easier to deny that the problem exists and to flee from it than to stand one's ground and work toward a mature level of interpersonal sharing and friendship. The women, on the other hand, look on the staff as a place to form relationships. They value them and put energy into staff interaction. Their desire for mutual sharing may be misconstrued by the priests as a desire for intimacy, when all they are seeking is mutual care, concern, and understanding.

Improving Collaborative Ministry

There are many practical methods for improving the level of communication and interaction between men and women on your parish staff or team. (See Chapter 5 for further suggestions.) To create a conducive environment for mutual sharing, you should first establish a tradition of regularly scheduling time during which tasks are put aside and staff members have a chance to speak freely about their feelings, frustrations, joys, and success. Encourage active listening without interruption. Give everyone time to tell her or his story. Rotate the leadership position so that the men on the staff— especially the pastor—are not always running these sharing sessions.

Be sure everyone, ordained and nonordained alike, has a clear job description. These descriptions should include how much time each member is expected to spend in staff interaction and collaboration and how much time each should spend in his or her area of ministry. Encourage all staff members to keep in touch with new directions and current trends in the Church. The staff should go as a group to workshops or seminars on communication, leadership, and decision-making skills. They will then be able to support one another in practicing the new techniques and insights gained at the training sessions.

Be visible as a group at parish functions so that parishioners see you working as a unit and not just as individuals. Celebrating liturgy as a staff on regular occasions and being present together at parish functions helps both the parish and the staff recognize that the staff is a corporate entity and not simply a collection of individual ministers.

Back each other up when a crisis arises. Don't let petty squabbles divide the staff. Tensions and conflicts are inevitable. They are signs of a group growing closer together. But don't let them destroy you. Use the crises as occasions for more honest and direct interaction. (Conflict management is discussed further in Chapter 5.)

Discuss the concepts important to you as a group: staff, team, intimacy, power, mutuality, authority, pastoring, and ministry to name but a few. Use pictures and images to keep the discussion from becoming just an intellectual exercise.

Realize that every time a new person joins the staff, the staff is a new group altogether. Whatever attempt was made previously at team building will have to be repeated, at least in an abbreviated form, so that the new person feels included and part of the group. This happens slowly. Allow a few months, at least, for the integration process to take hold.

Work toward providing job security for all nonordained members, either by establishing multi-year contracts or advocating diocesan personnel policies that include all professional parish ministers and not just priests. If the priests are given a regular period of tenure, why not other staff members?

Finally, the staff should set up a process of evaluation for all of its members, even the pastor. This evaluation process might include a yearly self-assessment, along with reports from other staff members and from parishioners who are affected by this person's area of ministry. The results of these assessments might go to a board, to the council, or to the staff itself for critique and final evaluation. This evaluation process can be a threatening experience, especially for the priests, who are not accustomed to this procedure. But as the tradition grows, those being evaluated will come to see it more as an affirmation of the good they have done than as a critique of what they have failed to accomplish.

Parish staffs, so essential to parish life and operation, are also undergoing a great deal of conflict and turmoil at present. No doubt the Spirit is in the midst of this struggle because much good is coming from the effort. One important change on parish staffs is the shift from a one-man show, with the pastor in charge, to a collaborative exercise of mutual ministry.

NOTES

1. Three of these types of leaders are discussed in the Management Design Institute, *Leadership: The Responsible Exercise of Power* (Cincinnati: Management Design, Inc., 1977), p. I-1.
2. Thomas Sweetser, *Successful Parishes: How They Meet the Challenge of Change* (Minneapolis: Winston Press, 1983), p. 29.
3. Carol Wisniewski Holden, *Report of Parish Teams* (Chicago: Parish Evaluation Project, 1985), p. 16-17.
4. Barbara Valuckas, SSND, "Staff Relationships," in *Gathering God's People*, ed. J. Stephen O'Brien (Huntington, Ind.: Our Sunday Visitor, 1982), p. 13-30. This essay discusses many of the same areas of misunderstanding that we have encountered in our work with parish staffs.

Further Reading

Gilligan, Carol. *In A Different Voice*. Cambridge: Harvard University Press, 1982.

Rockers, Dolore, OSF, Ph.D., and Kenneth J. Pierre, Ph.D. *Shared Ministry: An Integrated Approach to Leadership and Service.* Winona, Minn.: Saint Mary's Press, 1984.

Schaller, Lyle E. *Effective Church Planning.* Nashville: Abingdon Press, 1979.

Whitehead, James D., and Evelyn Eaton Whitehead. *Community of Faith.* New York: The Seabury Press, 1982.

Chapter 5

TEAM-BUILDING: STEPS TO SUCCESS

Since Vatican II there has been a trend toward more collaborative ministry in the Church. Parish staffs have been encouraged to spend time together sharing dreams about the future direction of the parish. Each staff member has taken on more responsibility as part of a group that models community for the rest of the parish.

Many staffs have tried implementing the concept of team ministry in their parishes, but some have met with frustration when their experience did not fulfill their ideal of team ministry. Individual members have different concepts of team ministry, which causes conflict and misunderstanding among members. Some ambivalence about team ministry also arises from lack of clearly defined roles and responsibilities. Yet our research proves that pastoral teams are becoming more prevalent in the Catholic Church.[1]

As early as 1970 team ministry was becoming a popular term in the American Catholic Church and various models were tried. In the Hartford and Boston areas, priests jointly shared responsibility for one parish. In the Louisville Diocese the parishioners were divided according to needs and interests. Individual priests pastored these areas, yet worked together as teams. In all three dioceses team ministry was carried out by the priests, not lay people.

In the early 1980s the concept of team ministry took on still another meaning. Professional lay staff members as well as the priest shared equal responsibility for a given parish. In some cases parishes didn't even have a resident pastor. The administrator and the pastoral associate conducted the day-to-day operation of the parish, while the pastor fulfilled his role in two or three parishes. This trend continues to the present day.

Although the concept of team ministry is becoming more of a reality in today's Church and is held up as the ideal style of leadership for the future, the Church as a whole is not yet at the point of complete acceptance. Because of our present leadership structures in the Church, dioceses, and parishes, an intermediate phase seems a necessary step before achieving a team ministry where all members share the responsibility equally. French and Bell, in *Organization Development*, define the process of deliberately creating a team as team-building.[2] The emphasis on deliberate efforts suggests something substantial that must be constructed in stages and will take time to complete.

This chapter discusses how to provide an environment for a parish staff to become a more cohesive team and to become more effective in parish ministry. But there is a distinction between working together as a team and doing team ministry. Chapter 4 provided a definition of team ministry in which all members share equal authority. Team-building is a process that facilitates the transition from a staff model, in which the pastor is the primary leader of the group, to a team model. In order to help staffs through the transition, the Parish Evaluation Project works with individual parishes. We encourage more interaction and sharing of responsibilities within them, whatever the leadership structure may be. All that is needed to assure positive results is members who are willing to attend the team-building sessions and make a commitment to the process. Use of an outside consultant is not essential but can be a rewarding experience.

The team-building process discussed in this chapter is based on our work with pastoral teams around the country. The following needs were most often mentioned by staff members:

1. To identify what each person means by a team approach.
2. To provide the occasion for people to share their expectations with other team members.
3. To clarify the roles and job descriptions of individual members.

4. To help people relate to each other in a healthy way, especially in dealing with conflict situations.

These needs can be addressed by emphasizing five aspects of group dynamics:

1. Faith Sharing
2. Collaboration
3. Variety of Gifts
4. Handling Conflict
5. Termination

This five-step process helps a staff become a better working group and facilitates an environment for sharing responsibility as parish ministers. As a group goes through the five steps, a spirit of trust and understanding is developed.

The first two sessions of the team-building process provide opportunities for individuals to share their experiences, look at group interaction, and clarify roles for members of the staff. The third session focuses on the wide variety of gifts that members bring to the group. The fourth session emphasizes coping with conflicts and using them as opportunities to grow and develop character. The fifth and final session helps teams deal with termination and also provides staffs with the means to evaluate how well they work as a group and to decide what changes need to be made. Prayer is also an important element of each session, setting the tone for the presentation.

We have developed five group sessions, each of which is based on one of the five aspects of group dynamics. The suggested time for each session is from three to five hours. Be sure to add stretch or coffee breaks to each session.

SESSION 1: FAITH SHARING

Focus: Sharing each person's development in and understanding of ministry in order to build a sense of community.

Process: Personal history lines and image of ministry.

Agenda: Prayer
History line
   Individual reflection
   Group sharing
Image of ministry
   Individual reflection
Identifying insights from session
Wrap-up

Parish staffs are composed of professional people who feel called to exercise some form of ministry. Realizing this, we try to set the tone for the first session by acknowledging people's gifts. To provide a conducive environment, we suggest a reading from the liturgy for Pentecost Sunday (Acts 2: 1–4).

Because this session emphasizes getting to know one another better, the group members are encouraged to reflect on their personal experience of God, Church, and ministry. How have these three elements been integrated in their lives? What were some significant moments in their lives that brought them to this place?

To help focus on those moments and to encourage sharing, we usually model our own history line for them. Using pieces of newsprint 3-by-2 feet in size, we draw a line to represent our lives from birth to the present day.

Date of birth   Today's date

Special periods, people, and events that brought us awareness of God, involvement in the Church, and commitment to specific areas of ministry are plotted along the line. While sharing the significance of these moments, we notice that these experiences may not have all been joyful. Sometimes crisis situations and critical decisions made after periods of discernment prompted moments of growth.

After we have finished sharing our stories, we invite all the staff members to spend ten minutes putting together their own history lines. We suggest they find a comfortable spot in the surrounding area that will provide an environment conducive to reflection.

Members of the staff then display their history line for everyone to see. With a spirit of trust and respect for confidentiality, they share their story with the rest of the group. Our experience of this sharing time has been intense and intimate. We have been overwhelmed with the stories of joys and sorrows, moments of togetherness and isolation. We always come away feeling energized by the experiences of other people and grateful that our paths have crossed.

After everyone has had a chance to share his or her story, the group reacts to the experience. Usually, members comment about the richness of one another's backgrounds and express the need to spend more time talking about some of the significant events in their lives. A spirit of trust begins to develop, and the group experiences a sense of communal bonding.

Because one common element of their history lines is ministry, we encourage the group to spend time thinking about this area. Staff members are asked to define the word *ministry* in symbolic terms. For example, ministry is like a kite. A kite comes in all shapes, sizes, and colors. Although it is attractive while on the ground, it becomes more exciting when it is in the air. It's free to move with the wind yet guided or controlled by a string. The string is usually held by a person who is anchored on the ground. The wind, an outside force, is necessary to put the kite in motion. Some movements are smooth as the kite is carried to great heights. At other times turbulence may cause the kite to dive or spin. In like manner, ministry comes in many shapes, sizes, and colors. It is attractive to look at but more exciting to do. It responds to shifts and changes in the environment but must be anchored in reality. It can, at times, be a soaring, lofty experience, while at other times, it can be frightening and confusing.

A volunteer is asked to share his or her image of ministry, offering no explanation of its meaning. It is important to make sure that everyone be familiar with the symbol. If not, the person is asked to describe it to the group. Other members of the staff are then encouraged to share how this image speaks to them of ministry. The person who volunteered the image is asked to listen to their explanations. Most of the time people add new concepts to the original thought, which helps everyone expand his or her under-standing of ministry. After several people have had a chance to respond, the person whose image has been discussed shares his or her initial thoughts on the image and tells what effect the comments of others have had on his or her concept of ministry.

Each person, in turn, goes through this experience. If the staff numbers more than six members, small groups of three or four are formed for the sharing of images. This portion of the session takes at least one half-hour. When all have had a chance to share their image in the small groups, they then reflect on what common elements they found in the images. This information is then shared with the larger group. Thus, the group has a chance to react as a whole and to experience a greater sense of bonding around the important issue of ministry.

During the last ten minutes of the session, we try to recap the entire session, and we invite the group to reflect on this experience. After some moments of quiet, the staff members are encouraged to share any reactions or insights they have garnered.

We have led such sessions with several staffs, and we have felt an intense closeness with the groups and are always amazed at the similarities in people's stories and understandings of ministry. The stories challenge the participants to take more risks and deepen their commitment to God. We have yet to experience a negative comment from a staff member about this experience. One staff member said he learned more about his eleven colleagues in this one session than he had in working with them for an entire year.

The first session of the team-building process powerfully orients new members of a staff and provides the occasion for old members to appreciate one another more. Having looked at each person as an individual, the group is now better able to examine its group characteristics.

Session 2: Collaboration

Focus: Clarifying different understandings of staff and team as well as each person's role and job description on staff.

Process: Framework of collaboration and differences between men and women.

Agenda: Prayer
Framework of collaboration
    Psychological and cultural influences
Men/Women differences
    Areas of staff interaction
People-Task Grid
    Individual reflection
    Group sharing
Stages of community growth
    Group sharing
Role and job descriptions
    Individual reflection
    Group sharing
Review of session
Wrap-up

At the beginning of this session, we ask the staff members to think of a situation in which they felt the Lord working through them. We encourage them to retrieve as much of the story as possible: who they were with, where and when the story took place, and what they said or did. After giving them a few minutes to think about this, we read sections from 1 Corinthians in which Paul speaks about being a co-worker of the Lord (1 Cor. 1:14–10; 3:4–11).

When the reading is finished, we ask staff members to pair up and share their stories. Five minutes later the group is called to a moment of silent reflection and then petitions are encouraged. Prayer is brought to a close with a *Glory Be*.

Framework of Collaboration

Our experience with parish staffs has caused us to include in this step in the team-building process some reflections on the dynamics of group interaction. When we speak of collaboration, we are mainly concerned with people, their history, and their contribution to the group. Because staffs are composed of men and women, ordained and nonordained, these individual differences along with other influences affect the way people interact.

There are several givens that groups need to be conscious of as they move toward collaboration and shared responsibility. Our presentation sums up these givens in two categories: (1) influences from within the group, and (2) influences from outside the group.

Psychological Influences

A staff member's degree of self-confidence contributes to the group's level of collaboration. If individual members are feeling good about themselves, their contribution to the group will be more life giving. They will be enthusiastic and supportive of others. They will be able to accept challenges from other members and risk learning something new. Members who lack self-confidence are usually overly sensitive to what others say regarding their area of ministry and may be paralyzed by fear when asked to move in new directions. Their lack of confidence affects the group not always in a visible way, but in undertones of dissatisfaction, pettiness, and immature behavior.

The different levels of motivation and desire to be part of the staff or team also affect collaborative efforts. It would be ideal if all staff members had the same level of commitment. But experience has proven that although some ministers are deeply committed to their work beyond the call of duty, others are only involved on a surface level. Efficiency in their own areas of ministry seems to be their goal, not sharing experiences of growth through staff interaction and working together to accomplish successful programs.

The different roles and positions held by staff members also affect interaction. Some roles on the staff may have greater authority associated with them. The pastor, for example, may use his position of power stemming from the hierarchical model of leadership so prevalent in the Church before Vatican II. On the other hand, a pastor trying to exercise a shared ministry by encouraging the staff to work as a team may be criticized by his parishioners because he does not take charge. People generally want to know who the leader is. As a result they may force a pastor into a position of authority with which they are more comfortable. Full-time staff members may wield more authority than part-time staff members, or professional ministers more than secretaries and clerical workers. Uncertainty about the way people fit into the staff and about the positions they hold influences collaboration.

The previous experience of the staff as a whole and of each individual on the staff also affects collaborative efforts. Staff members have their own stories to tell. Some members have been working in the same parish for several years. Their programs may have been successful and affirmed by the parishioners. This gives them a sense of ownership and can foster a sense of security or even complacency. Other staff members may have experienced uncomfortable situations in which they did not live up to the expectations of the parishioners and therefore feel insecure.

People's past experience affects the way they will handle new situations. The success stories give energy and hope to build dreams for the future, but the painful events may dampen enthusiasm and instill scepticism and fear instead. For example, the lay principal on staff may have come from a parish in which his contract wasn't renewed because the parish wanted a nun to take over. He may carry that insecurity with him into the new situation and wonder if he will be replaced again.

Other contributing influences are the different types of religious experience and theological emphases each person brings to the staff. In one parish the staff found it difficult to pray together because a few of the members, who were participating in charismatic renewal, felt that prayer time should be spent invoking the Holy Spirit and speaking in tongues. Other members found this difficult. Thus, the staff was unable to pray as a group.

Some staff members might favor a servant model of Church that emphasizes the need to care for the poor and homeless. They might suggest that the former convent be used to shelter the homeless or that more of the parish budget be used for feeding and clothing the hungry. This may stir up some emotion among staff members who feel more attention should be given to the parish's spiritual needs, especially to the sacramental programs and to religious education. These staff members may argue that the parishioners come first and that the staff wouldn't have space for its own meetings if the convent were used by outsiders. Helping staffs to accept diversity and then to build on their commonalities fosters an environment in which collaboration can be achieved.

Even the surrounding environment affects how staff members interact. For example, what can one expect to accomplish in an inner-city parish if the funds and morale of the people are at a level of bare survival? In such a situation most of the staff's energy is used to deal with the parishioners' struggles, and little is left over for their interaction with other staff members. In a suburban area, however, a person may find that he or she is one of a number of people working as co-ministers on a parish staff. Many resources are available to them. Their problem may be that parishioners have too many interests elsewhere. The parish is the last place parishioners want to look for involvement. These staff members must struggle to find a way to tap the self-interest of the parishioners, and this is a difficult task.

The preceding examples demonstrate that staff members and the way they relate to each other are affected by the larger environment. But they are affected by the immediate surroundings as well. Examine staff meetings: Where are they held? Who runs the meetings? How are decisions made? Do members share ideas or just give reports? Do they have a chance to socialize with one another?

Answers to the above questions give some insight into the way collaboration is exercised on the local level. Thus, it might help collaboration if meetings were held on neutral territory rather than in the rectory (the priests' territory), or the school (the principal's territory). Whether or not the group recognizes it, a person carries more weight in the decision-making process if the meeting is held on his or her turf. A good environment for prayer, decision making, sharing of ideas, and socializing fosters a spirit of collaboration.

The seasons of the year and the pressures of time also affect collaboration. We don't always have the luxury of unlimited time. Staff members have different commitments. Those involved in RCIA have more demands placed on them before the Easter season. The principal of the school may find it difficult to attend staff meetings during school hours. Staff members with families experience tension between the responsibilities of home and parish ministry. Seasons of the year make a difference. It is difficult to plan a relaxed staff day two weeks before the Christmas holidays. In January and

February people find their energy and enthusiasm lagging, while spring revitalizes people as they turn their attention to summer vacation. Time and seasons, in other words, affect people in both positive and negative ways, and knowing the difference can facilitate collaboration.

Cultural Influences

Our culture is struggling with changing relationships. The changing relations between men and women demonstrate this most effectively. Opportunities for women to achieve success and status not only in the academic world, but also in the professional world have become more numerous and acceptable. People are no longer surprised when a woman becomes an executive director of a prominent company. The stereotype of the woman who is supposed to be a mother, fulfilling domestic duties while being available and supportive to her husband when he returns home from work, is being called into question.

Men are developing their feminine qualities and consider it an accomplishment in self-sufficiency when they can care for their own domestic needs. Taking turns in being house-parent and rearing the children is common in families today. Couples share more of the mundane activities as well as sharing the role of breadwinner.

Our culture has also experienced a shift in how it understands leadership. We are moving away from a hierarchical model to a team model of leadership in all areas: business, education, and government. Employees are encouraged to give input for improving production or increasing efficiency. Many organizations and businesses have introduced the team concept where several people work together to ensure the best results. This cultural emphasis is having a profound effect on parish staffs.

Staffs must work through Church structures. At the same time it is difficult to have a good experience of collaboration if the Church continues to reinforce the autocratic model in which the ordained members exercise a heavy hand. So long as people are set apart by roles rather than considered as equals among others, collaboration may be difficult.

Rules and regulations sometimes get in the way of the Spirit. Staffs find themselves bound by authority and limited by Church law in expressing their giftedness. For example, present structure and regulation dictate that one's sex determines whether or not one can hold the office of pastor.

Within each parish people's needs and expectations are often vastly different. Some parishioners, for example, assume that since staff members are professionals, they should be able to handle everything on their own. In response to such an attitude, some staffs develop messiah complexes and overextend themselves, while others despair.

Parish history and traditions can also be a source of pressure. No one wants things to die. "But we have always done it this way!" becomes the rallying cry. Much effort is exerted to keep "it" alive even if "it" has lost its meaning.

But traditions can also be the source for pulling the parish together. If looked at in a positive way, the time and energy used to maintain parish traditions can be an enriching experience.

After we have presented this information on the influences exerted on collaboration from within and outside the group, we focus on a previously mentioned element that influences collaboration: sex role differences. Although the differences are somewhat stereotyped, men and women relate differently to various situations. At this point in the session, we present the material described in "Collaboration between Men and Women" in Chapter 4 and discuss the five areas in which confusion and misunderstanding are most pronounced: personal sharing, accountability, performance, definition of team, and sexuality.

This information gives the staff a great deal to think about. But reflecting on sex role differences is not enough. If the staff is truly concerned about fostering better collaboration, it is necessary for personal sharing to take place.

A common tool for analyzing group interaction is the People-Task Grid (see Figure 1 in Chapter 4). After listening to the presentation on the meaning of the grid, each staff member is asked to draw an outline of the grid on a 3-by-5 index card. We ask members to place an X on the grid in the spot that best describes the present level of staff interaction as they see it. They are then asked to put an O in the spot that best describes the level of interaction they desire for the group.

We then draw the People-Task Grid on a large piece of newsprint or poster paper. Staff members are invited to place their X in the chosen spot and explain the reason for choosing this position.

When everyone is finished placing an X on the newsprint, the staff as a whole draws conclusions from the configuration of the Xs. In some cases the Xs may have been grouped together, showing that the staff agrees on the present level of interaction. In others, the Xs are scattered on the grid, revealing disparate perceptions. Members are asked to repeat the process by placing an O on the newsprint along with an explanation for choosing this position. An example of a staff's People-Task Grid is given in Figure 3.

When this exercise is completed, the group discusses what a realistic goal for their interaction might be. In order to reach the goal, some behavior modification may be necessary. The group is encouraged to come to some consensus about whatever changes

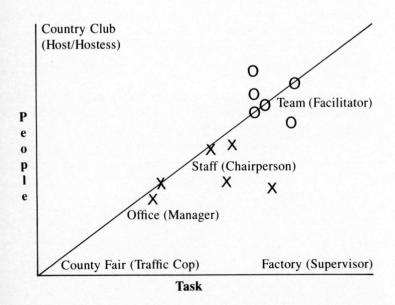

Figure 3. Staff Perceptions Plotted on a People/Task Grid

may be necessary in the group's patterns of collaboration in order to achieve its goal.

While working with parish staffs and teams, we have discovered that a majority of the Xs are clustered around the staff level of the grid or toward the Task axis. The position of most Os, however, indicates that people want to move closer to the team model and that they desire to spend more time interacting with one another. Some members are concerned about getting too familiar with each other, not wishing to make a commitment to friendship. Others stress the need to develop closer ties with one another to improve the image of shared ministry in the parish.

Having studied their level of interaction, we then ask the staff to look at any other dynamics at work in their group. First, they reflect on the chart shown in Figure 4, which describes the stages of community growth. Next, each member is asked to identify the stage at which he or she belongs as an individual and which stage best describes the group as a whole.

Individual sharing is important at this point. The group is encouraged to listen attentively to each member. Comments by the participants have been enlightening. New members often identify with the orientation stage, while older members find themselves at the conflict or faith-sharing stage. Occasionally, some of the older staff members also find that they are still at the orientation stage of the chart. Others feel they have gone through a number of these stages several times, deepening the level of investment. Seldom do we hear a group say it has experienced the termination phase. Staff members may have left in the past, but the staff may never have dealt with this stage. (For this reason we have added this phase as the final session of the team-building process.)

Dialogue helps the group clarify its future direction and the stages of community growth through which it needs to move. With some staffs, we shorten the time of discussion, knowing that they are capable of handling this chart on their own.

Thus far the second session has focused on individual and group interaction. But the reason the group is together is to perform a ministry within the parish. Some staff members find that their jobs overlap with other staff members or that they begin to accumulate extra jobs that may eventually lead to burnout. Thus, clarifying

Stages of Community Groups

Stage	Predominant Feeling	How the Feeling is Expressed	What You Can Do
1. Orientation	Insecurity	Talking Getting clarity Silence Questioning whether this group meets my needs	Clarify norms, expectations, etc.
2. Inclusion	Fear of exclusion	Do I belong? Will I be accepted? Am I different? Fear of doing something that will get me rejected	Find ways of including everyone Encourage asking questions
3. Control	Competitiveness	How can I be important in this group? Who is most important? Why?	Focus on the unique value of each person Decrease differences Focus on commonality
4. Conflict	Tension	Fight Nonattendance Regression Denial of the problem	Raise the conflict issue and deal with it
5. Cohesion	Relaxation	Lots of interaction Concern for one another Accomplishment of tasks	Make sure the group is moving toward its purpose
6. Faith Sharing	Peacefulness	Honest sharing Trust	Make sure people feel comfortable
7. Intimacy	Ambivalence	How close do I want to get to these people? Approach-avoidance	Discover a comfortable level without feeling guilty
8. Termination	Avoidance	Attempt to avoid the end	Deal with your feelings

Figure 4. Reprinted, by permission, from Loughlan Sofield and Rosine Hammett, *Inside Christian Community* (New York: Le Jacq Publishing, Inc., 1981), p. 14.

their own roles and job descriptions and sharing them with the entire group gives individuals an opportunity to let go of menial tasks and concentrate on those they are better prepared to handle.

We facilitate this by means of the role and job description sheets. Each member is asked to fill out the job description sheet shown in Figure 5. *All* items for which they are responsible are to be listed in the left-hand column. In the middle column, staff members rate their level of satisfaction. In the right-hand column they indicate who would be the ideal person to perform the task.

Job Description

1. High	1. Self
2. Medium	2. Other Staff
3. Low	3. Secretary
	4. Council/Committee
	5. Parishioner
	6. Other
	7. No one

Item (What I do)	*Satisfaction*	*Ideal Performer*
1.		.
2.		.

Figure 5. Job Description Sheet

After completing the job description sheet, individuals fill in the role description sheet shown in Figure 6, which has places for the names of all the other staff members. Taking each of the other staff members in turn, they write down what the role of the individual is, what they think that person is now doing, and what they think would be the ideal.

Role Description

What you think is happening now.	What you think would be the ideal.
Name:	
Name:	

Figure 6.   Role Description Sheet

If the staff is larger than six people, we divide the group so that each person is assigned three others for the role description sheet. This portion of the exercise takes twenty to thirty minutes. When the staff has completed both worksheets, the group shares the results by means of the following process:

Preparation: Put as many pieces of newsprint on the wall as there are staff members. It is good to have one person facilitate this process and fill in the following information on the newsprint while everyone else is listening.

1. One person volunteers to talk about his or her role. Put that person's name at the top of the newsprint.
2. Using a black marker, write down all the things *other* people listed for this individual.
3. The individual then points out which of these items were not on his or her list. Using a green marker, put an asterisk in front of these items.
4. With a red marker, add all the other items the individual has on his or her list that are not listed on the newsprint.

5. With a blue marker, put a plus ($+$) before each item that causes the greatest satisfaction.
6. With a blue marker, put a minus ($-$) before each item that causes the least satisfaction.
7. With an arrow ($\rightarrow$), mark the items the individual would like to give away to someone else.
8. Taking into account this job description, the group discusses the person's role for the future. Using a green marker, fill in a statement about the future role.

Staff members can then trade items with one another if they wish. Individuals have experienced this exercise as a moment of freedom because it allowed them to let go of jobs without feeling guilty. This process is effective either at the beginning or end of the academic year as staffs plan for the future. Members have felt relieved and supported as their colleagues affirmed their work and encouraged them to pursue new tasks in the future.

Before concluding the second session, we ask participants for their reactions. What were some of the insights they gleaned from the day or the high and low points of the experience? The group's reaction helps us evaluate the session and provides possibilities for future adjustments.

Session 3. Variety of Gifts

Focus: Discovering how people approach the same situation in different ways.

Process: The Myers-Briggs Type Indicator as applied to staff interaction.

Agenda: Prayer
Overview of Myers-Briggs types
Reading of individual profiles
Describing personal preferences
What can be gained from other types
Group sharing
Review session
Wrap-up

Before this session, all staff members fill out a Myers-Briggs

Type Indicator supplied by the Parish Evaluation Project.[3] When the tests are scored, indicating the personality type of each staff member, we prepare sheets describing the general functions of each person's personality. This session opens with a reading from Romans, Chapter 12, verses 4 through 8, describing the importance of different gifts.

Excitement mounts as the staff gathers together for the third session and its focus on the rich variety of gifts present in the group. This rich diversity of gifts is one of the elements that often causes tension. People work in different ways. They also expect others to think and feel the same way they do. One way to ease group tension and facilitate better interaction among staff members is to clarify and discuss individual differences.

Following prayer some general information is given about the Myers-Briggs Type Indicator. Convinced of the value of function types, or psychological types, defined by Carl Jung, Isabel Briggs Myers, in collaboration with her mother, Katherine C. Briggs, developed in 1942 what is now called the Myers-Briggs Type Indicator. Use of the instrument was limited until the 1970s when there was a growing interest in applying it to personal evaluation, vocational counseling, student counseling, employment, and marriage counseling. Recently, it has been used in many ministerial training programs and for parish staff counseling. The instrument has demonstrated its value by affirming self-understanding and worth. It measures people's preference in different areas. Staff members learn that one preference is not better than another, but simply different.

We begin our presentation by focusing on four areas: (1). the way we relate to our world, (2). the way we gather information, (3) the way we make decisions, and (4) the way we act things out. First, regarding the way we relate to the world, the instrument helps us recognize how some people have a preference for extroversion (E): an orientation to the outer world, to people and things. Others have a preference for introversion (I): an orientation primarily to the inner world, to concepts and ideas.

Second, the instrument measures the preferential way in which one perceives or gathers information. Sensing (S) types of people predominantly use their senses to gather facts. Intuitive (N) types of people primarily search for meanings, relationships, and possibilities beyond the reach of the senses.

Third, the instrument demonstrates how people make decisions in different ways. Some people primarily use their thinking (T), logically and analytically moving toward a decision. Other people primarily make their decisions on the basis of feeling (F), or personal values.

Finally, the instrument measures the various ways different people act on their decisions. Some people judge (J), usually preferring to come to closure or decisions on the matters at hand. Other people prefer to keep things open, continuing to adapt and look at the possibilities. This is called the perceptive function (P).

After listening to our presentation, staff members guess what combination of functions they perceive themselves to use. The make-up of the staff personality types is then displayed on newsprint. For example, it may look something like the following:

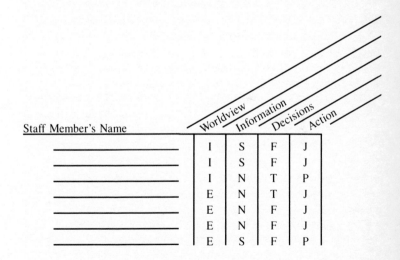

Staff Member's Name	Worldview	Information	Decisions	Action
_____	I	S	F	J
_____	I	S	F	J
_____	I	N	T	P
_____	E	N	T	J
_____	E	N	F	J
_____	E	N	F	J
_____	E	S	F	P

Each member is given his or her Myers-Briggs score sheet, along with the explanation of his or her profile. Generally, we give the people fifteen minutes to read their profiles. While reading, they are asked to keep in mind some aspects of the description that best describes them. It is natural for individuals to agree with some of the elements of the description about themselves but to question others. Then we invite the group members to identify themselves on the newsprint. As they do so we add their name to the chart.

As we continue to share more information about the various preferences, staff members begin to discover why there may be tensions among them. Some of the members may be extroverts (E) who like to think out loud and reflect later, while others may be introverts (I) who need time to reflect before speaking. The extroverts wonder why the introverts are quiet and hesitant to speak. Introverts are looking for some space to think, and then hope they get the opportunity to speak.

The sensing (S) types are concerned with the facts and want to know the details. The intuitive (N) types are always looking for more possibilities for parish programs and for making connections with other opportunities. The sensing types wonder when the intuitives are finally going to get practical. The intuitives feel that the sensing types lack vision.

The thinking (T) types are people who analyze the matter at hand and then logically work out answers. The feeling (F) types are people who balance their personal values with the need for harmony in the group; thus, logical answers are not their primary concerns. The judging types (J) are people who work hard to get things decided. Their motto is "We can't keep floating forever." The perceiving (P) or adapting types are people who do not look for quick closure. Rather, they try to keep the discussion open to other and new possibilities. Their motto is, "Let's not settle things too quickly."

The thinkers are frustrated with the feeling types, because the latter can't explain why they think the way they do. The feeling types are frustrated with the thinkers because the thinkers seem to lack compassion and sensitivity to feelings. The judging types are frustrated because the adapters don't come to closure. The adapting types are frustrated because the judging types want to close prematurely. All of us have experienced the frustration of working in groups. Our natural tendency is to prefer that others would work as we do. But if such were the case, much would be lacking in the group. Parish staffs or teams need to be made up of all the varying types.[4]

The Myers-Briggs instrument does not claim to be perfect, only indicative. Thus, it is important to realize that people do change and are influenced by their environment. Therefore, a person whose score showed that he or she was an ESFJ today may show him or her to be a ENFJ one year from now. Why? If, for example, over the past year the person was responsible for getting the parish census compiled and computerized, he or she was involved in a tedious, factual job. The person had to be precise about details, and therefore, his or her sensing (S) preference grew stronger. The following year the person may be on a committee planning a parish renewal. The committee is looking at all the possibilities for parish participation, evaluating whether large or small group activities will be more effective, and brainstorming to determine what resources are available to meet their desired outcome. This experience will reinforce the individual's intuitive (N) preference. Both activities described here require information gathering, but the former requires facts or statistics while the latter requires dreaming and searching for possibilities.[5]

After reviewing their profiles, staff members take turns describing their strengths to the group. Since no one has a copy of anyone else's profile, we encourage staff members to describe their preferences in detail. We also encourage them to share the areas in which they feel they need help from other types within the group. This discussion time is the most important part of the session. It is best to have an outside consultant familiar with the Myers-Briggs instrument to facilitate this discussion, for the insight of an objective person is most helpful. In our experience, groups have used this session to reconcile differences and to gain new insight into previous conflict situations. Understanding individuals' preferences does not eliminate the tensions among staff members, but it does help create a more accepting, conciliatory environment.

When all have had a chance to share their profiles and discuss their own and other people's gifts, we bring the session to a close by again reflecting on what took place within the group. Staff members may want to focus their reflections on themselves as individuals or on the group as a whole. Those who wish to are invited to share these reflections with the entire group.

The Myers-Briggs Type Indicator points out individual preferences as they relate to varying situations. Although we have stressed the positive aspects of the preferences, some people may tend to see these preferences as negative areas of their personality. Staffs need to counter this tendency and help individual members recognize and understand that one preference (or set of preferences) is not better than another. Staffs must also resist categorizing individual members, insisting that they are "always" this or that way. Thus, we always remind staffs that individuals can and do change.

No matter how much knowledge we have about our personalities, however, when two or more people interact with each other, there is bound to be some conflict. And conflict can be destructive if not handled properly. Sadly, most of the time, conflict is not handled properly. Why? People lack the skills to cope with conflicts and to grow through conflict.

Session 4. Handling Conflict

Focus: Looking at limits to staff effectiveness both as individuals and as a group.

Process: Conflict management and avoiding burnout.

Agenda: Prayer
Reflect on personal experience of conflict
Ways of managing conflict
    Win/Lose
    Accommodation
    Avoidance
    Compromise
Reflect on personal experience
Degree of difficulty in managing conflict
Share insights with another person
Win/Win style
Progression of burnout
Review of session
Wrap-up

Wherever two or more people gather and share ideas, the possibility exists for misunderstanding and frustration. Since this was true even among the Apostles, we begin our focus on our limitations with a scriptural reading from Acts (15:1–3, 6–12) in which we discover how Paul and Barnabas dealt with a conflict situation. Following the reading, staff members are invited to share petitions or other prayers. The prayer portion of the session concludes with the Lord's Prayer.

The first part of the session addresses conflict management. We ask individuals to reflect on a situation that caused some conflict with another member of the staff and to write on an index card as many of the details about the event as they can remember: who was involved, what the conflict was about, and how it was handled. Their reflections on their personal experience provide a practical application for the general information we present on conflict management.

The index cards are put aside as we present information about conflict management. We avoid the term *conflict resolution*, because it implies that a conflict situation can be resolved. This is rarely the case. *Conflict management* seems to be a more realistic term because at least one party involved in a conflict needs to negotiate to bring about acceptance by the other.

Our own perceptual framework structures the world for us. We make sense out of reality by interpreting our experiences so that they fit into the framework we regard as meaningful. In *Resolving Church Conflicts* G. Douglass Lewis defines the components of human action:

The activity of one's life seeks to fulfill this set of *needs*. In order to fulfill these needs, a person works towards *goals*. Goals are states of being that do not now exist but that we can imagine existing. For example, I cannot play the piano but I can imagine myself playing one someday if I take lessons and practice. In other words, goals are targets toward which we direct our actions. These actions are called *behavior*. The diagram [see Figure 7] shows a goal coming before behavior, even though behavior is the movement towards a goal. The diagram merely illustrates that a goal—something towards which behavior is moving—must be anticipated, though not accomplished, before behavior is activated.

The model also recognizes that persons have an automatic *internal feedback* process that operates at every step of the cycle. When a goal is achieved, internal feedback checks to see if achieving the goal really fulfilled the need or not. At the behavioral level, there is feedback as to whether or not that behavioral pattern really achieved the desired goal.

Whether something satisfies or not can only be determined by the individual who experiences it.[6]

Lewis also concludes that to be human involves three unavoidable realities: (1) the individual alone chooses the goal and behaviors; (2) the choice is made on the basis of what the individual sees is right from her or his perspective at that time; and (3) the individual determines whether the results are satisfying or not. One goal may, in fact, satisfy several needs, and one set of behaviors may be designed to accomplish several goals.[7]

Conflicts arise when we try to achieve our goals while interacting with other people who have also set goals for themselves. This is where the relationships indicated in Figure 7 come into play. Human

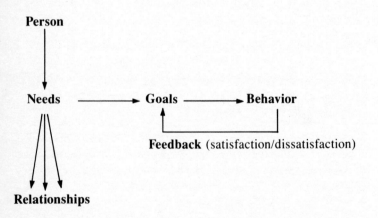

Figure 7.   Sources of Conflict: Goals versus Relationships

Adapted from G. Douglass Lewis, *Resolving Church Conflict* (San Francisco: Harper & Row, 1981), 10–11; reprinted by permission.

needs are satisfied by achieving one's goals or choosing a relationship. In order to protect a relationship, people will sometimes give up a goal. At other times, if the goal is deemed more important, the relationship takes second place. This creates conflict. The following case study portrays a conflict.

Case Study:

Kristen, the director of religious education at St. Thaddeus Parish, is planning a Lenten series for the adult education program. Having contacted several speakers for the evening events, she is inspired by the enthusiasm of some advisors to expand the program themes into the Sunday liturgies. The parish finished the RENEW program last year. The experience was so good, especially the Sunday liturgies, that she wants to create her program as a follow-up to RENEW. Some parishioners who were part of the small groups of RENEW think this is just what St. Thaddeus needs for this year.

Mark, the liturgy and music director, does not share Kristen's enthusiasm, especially since his liturgy committee has already done some brainstorming on the themes to be used for the Sundays during Lent. These themes are very different from Kristen's. The liturgy committee feels that the RENEW experience of the last three years was very effective, and they want to build on their past success. The committee believes that this is just what St. Thaddeus needs.

Here we have two qualified staff members, planning and dreaming for the future and responding to what each feels is best for the parishioners. The problem is that both ministers are planning for the same group of parishioners. Kristen is moving into Mark's territory, liturgy planning, creating conflict.

Although some committee members are involved with both staff members, for the purpose of handling the conflict, this analysis concentrates only on the two staff members. Two questions face Kristen and Mark: (1) How important is it to achieve my goal? (2) How important is my relationship with the other person involved? The answers to these questions determine how they will deal with the conflict. Four styles of managing conflict are presented in the following scenarios.[8]

The Win/Lose Style

The *win/lose* style is characterized by a concern for achieving one's goal even to the point of damaging the relationship with the other person. The achiever wins at all costs. This results in an aggressive, dogmatic, and inflexible approach to conflict management. Using the Myers-Briggs types of personalities, which we discussed in the previous session, we can say that the sensing (S) and judging (J) types and some thinking (T) types are most prone to using this style of conflict management.

Scenario

At the staff meeting Kristen presents her Lenten program with the idea of using it as a follow-up to RENEW. She has planned the program in detail and by now her excitement is so contagious that all the other staff members are becoming enthusiastic as well.

All, that is, except Mark. He tries to explain that the liturgy committee has already been working on themes for Lent. When one of the staff members asks if they have finished planning the liturgies in detail, he responds, "No, they are not complete. We just decided on which themes would be used. None of the details are worked out as yet."

At this point, Kristen suggests how much easier it would be for his committee if it were to decide to accept her program, which is already planned. The rest of the staff agrees. "Let's go with Kristen's program, Mark. It will save you a lot of time and energy."

Mark knows he is outnumbered. There is nothing he can say to change their minds. He is angry and feels defeated.

In this situation Kristen achieves her goal, but with no consideration for Mark's feelings. Mark loses this time, but he is thinking to himself that next time he will win.

The Accommodating Style

The *accommodating* style is characterized by a concern for preserving the relationship even at the price of giving up one's goal. The relationship is of utmost importance. However, in some situations there may be an assumption that the relationship is so fragile that the other party can't tolerate any conflict. People who tend toward the accommodating style are those who need harmony and affirmation. The extrovert (E) and feeling (F) types lean toward this style of conflict management. If people tend to accommodate too often, however, they begin to play the martyr's role. "Why do I always have to give in?" they say. But they have to remember that they are the ones who choose their behavior. they have no one to blame but themselves.

Scenario

Becoming aware of Mark's anger at the staff meeting, Kristen decides to stay on his good side because he helps her with the special liturgies for First Communion and Confirmation. She remembers how much time he spends with the children teaching them new songs in preparation for these celebrations. It is more important to her to have a good working relationship with him than to get excited about this Lenten program. Besides, she realizes how much time and work will be required for the program to be successful. She will have enough to do in preparing six evenings of adult formation with speakers and small groups.

Although staff members are siding with Kristen, she decides to hold off on the liturgy portion of the Lenten series and to focus on the speaker's series during the week. Mark is much relieved.

In this scenario Kristen thinks more of the relationship, so she accommodates by giving up a portion of her goal. To carry this even further, in many situations the accommodating person gives up the entire goal. It would not be surprising if Kristen were to say, "Mark, because you and your committee are concerned about continuing the RENEW model, why don't you plan the small group adult portion of the program as well." She would, of course, say this with some emotion.

The Avoidance Style

The *avoidance* style of conflict management is characteristic of individuals who are pessimistic about conflict. They view conflict as destructive to a relationship, and they cannot accomplish their goals in a conflict situation. Persons who use the avoidance or flight technique withdraw to avoid conflict. Sometimes people run away from situations psychologically by tuning out a conversation that causes the conflict. At a staff meeting one person may begin to daydream while a specific topic is being discussed. When the conversation changes he or she becomes an active participant once again, unaffected by what was previously said. As far as the person is concerned, the conflict-provoking topic never came up. At times individuals will even physically remove themselves to avoid a conflict situation or a person who might cause conflict. Let's look again at Kristen and Mark's situation.

Scenario

Mark notices that Kristen will be describing her Lenten program as a follow-up to RENEW. He is uncomfortable in dealing with conflict situations, so he can choose to handle the staff meeting in one of two ways. Mark can either find an excuse for not going to the meeting, or he can appear for the meeting but participate in a passive way. When Kristen brings up the Lenten program, he can show no signs of agreement or disagreement. His silence will be seen by the others as an acceptance of Kristen's program.

Behavior like this is sometimes overlooked or unnoticed if the staff does not use a consensus style of decision-making. Too often decisions are made after the staff has heard from the more vocal participants assuming indifference of those who have abstained from any discussion.

Because Mark did not deal with the conflict, he may walk away from the meeting questioning his position on the staff, especially as it pertains to his areas of expertise, liturgy and music. Mark's anger will force him to try harder to make sure he wins next time.

The Compromise Style

The *compromise* style of conflict management espouses the philosophy, "give a little, get a little." People use this style when they realize they cannot achieve their goal and still preserve the relationship. This is a political model: "Work for as much as you can get without jeopardizing something that may help you in the future." Compromise does help people manage conflict situations, but neither party is totally satisfied.

Scenario

Both Kristen and Mark have a chance to share their ideas at the staff meeting. It seems that both programs have themes that are of interest to the entire parish. Sister Irene, the school principal, suggests combining the best of both programs. Mark says he is willing to meet with Kristen to discuss the possibilities. Kristen is open to new options as long as some of her ideas will be accepted.

In a compromise situation Kristen and Mark are willing to work on the project together. After future discussions, it may turn out that some of Kristen's themes are used as well as some of Mark's. This compromise, however, is not accomplished without the cost of letting go. A lot of time and energy have already been invested by both staff members and their committees in order to come up with their original ideas. The advantage in using a compromise approach is that both Mark and Kristen achieve some of their goals, and their relationship is preserved.

These four styles of dealing with conflict may not be the best, but they are the ones used most often in the immediate conflict situation. Our emotions usually take over too quickly and cause some type of reaction.

The Win/Win Style

Conflict can be dealt with in an alternative way that preserves the goals of both individuals and not only maintains, but also strengthens the relationship between them. This alternative is the *win/win* style. Before explaining this fifth option, we ask the staff to look at the index cards they prepared at the beginning of the session. They then write down which of the four styles presented so far was used in the situation they recorded on the index cards.

Next, we look at the grid shown in Figure 8. The time axis designates the amount of time it takes to manage a conflict; the degree of difficulty axis measures the increasing difficulty of managing the conflict. The increasing investment of time and effort needed to manage a conflict can be plotted as a diagonal on this grid.

Figure 8 also demonstrates that conflicts can take place over facts. Each person may have a different set of facts or a different perception of the facts. This type of conflict takes the least amount of time and is not as difficult to manage. Sometimes people just forget about the conflict and move on. For example, the two of us had a conflict over facts. We disagreed over what time we should reassemble the small groups into the large hall for reports. Carol

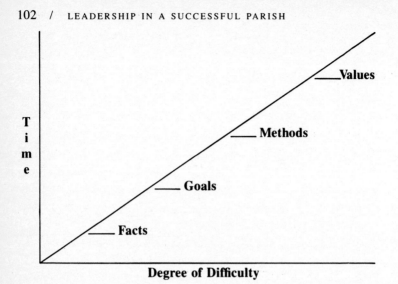

Figure 8. Levels of Conflict

thought the groups should be called together at ten minutes after the hour, Tom at fifteen minutes after the hour. The conflict was managed when we discovered each of us had a different time on our watches. We were making a decision based on different facts. Granted, this was a small matter, but until we discovered the source of the conflict, we experienced some impatience and frustration with each other.

Conflicts also can occur because of a different set of goals. In the case of Kristen and Mark, it took time and some energy to handle the conflict over differing goals for the Lenten program. Although there may be no problem in setting goals, the method by which the goals are to be achieved may cause some conflict. For example, if Mark and Kristen were united in their goal of providing a follow-up for RENEW, they could still have conflicts over how this could be accomplished. Kristen might want to use only the small group structure, while Mark might want to focus on the weekend liturgies. Even more time is required to deal with conflicts over methods, and people will also experience greater difficulty handling the situation.

The greatest degree of difficulty is faced when conflicts occur because of differing values. At this level it is almost impossible to manage the conflict. Values are so deeply held and so important to people that it is unlikely they can compromise them. The best way to handle this type of conflict is to bring it down to the level of goals or facts. Only then can some headway be made. For example, suppose Father Thomas Michaels, the pastor at St. Lawrence parish, has a conflict with Elaine, the pastoral associate. She advocates the view that women should be ordained as priests. She and Father Thomas may not agree on this issue at the value level. Right now, however, Elaine is concerned with the fact of having all women lectors at the Mother's Day liturgies, and Father Thomas can sympathize with her concern. Thus, they can bring the conflict down to a level they can handle.

Once the levels of conflict have been explained, staff members are encouraged to look at their personal conflict cards once again and to answer the following questions: Why did the conflict occur? Was it because of a difference in facts, goals, methods, or values? After writing some notes on the index card, staff members choose partners and spend twenty minutes sharing their conflict situations and the insights gained during the presentation. Some staff members choose for their partner the person with whom they had the conflict. Because both people listened to the same input they find it easier to talk about their conflict.

When we work with a group, instead of using the case of Kristen and Mark, we often describe some conflict situations that we ourselves experienced with each other while working as a team. Our way of handling the situations were not always the best, but we learned from the experiences. Laughing at our own mistakes is a good model for the group and helps them to risk being more open with one another. At least, they are willing to try. When the sharing time is completed, staff members come together and share their insights with the group.

We then turn to the alternative option for managing conflict, the win/win style, which we consider to be the best style. With a little practice staff members can achieve this level of conflict management. The win/win style combines a high level of concern for accomplishing one's personal goals while still preserving and even enhancing the relationship. It means treating the other person's goals with the same seriousness as one's own. Then, while working together, both people build a trust and openness so that both can share dreams and hopes.

Before anyone attempts to manage a conflict using the win/win style, one question must be asked and answered: "Who has the conflict?" A way of determining this is to ask a further question: "Who has the emotion?" The person with the emotion is the one who has the conflict. It is important to secure this information; the answer determines which strategy to use in a win/win situation. Managing a conflict situation in this way also presupposes a desire to take risks. A person can never be sure of the outcome. In order to manage conflict by means of the win/win style, four different skills are necessary in response to differing situations.

Someone else has a conflict with you

Scenario

At the staff meeting Kristen is unaware of Mark's conflict with her program. Only when he began to speak did she realize from the tone of his voice that he was angry.

Skill

If Kristen were using the win/win style, Mark's anger would be a signal for her to do some *creative, active listening.* She can try to uncover what bothers Mark. She may ask him how he feels about what she has presented. Or, picking up on his quiet passive behavior, she may ask him if he has any comments about what was just presented. After listening to Mark, Kristen may become aware of his feelings of anger at what he perceives as an attempt to take over a part of his area of ministry. She may find out that three of his committee members gave up going to a professional basketball game last Thursday so they could have a meeting to decide on the themes for the Lenten program.

You have a conflict with someone else

Scenario

As Kristen continues sharing her ideas at the staff meeting, Mark becomes aware of his frustration. He knows he has the emotion. What can he do to make this a win/win situation?

Skill

Mark can employ the skill of the *"I" statements*. This may be done at the time of the conflict or after he distances himself from the immediate situation and has time to think about what has happened. Mark might schedule a time to talk to Kristen and proceed with the following three steps:

1. *State the concrete situation.* "*I* was present for the staff meeting when you explained your plans for the Lenten program."

Mark does not bring in any other problem areas with Kristen, but concentrates on this one situation.

2. *Tell your feelings.* Mark tells Kristen, "*I* was angry and hurt. *I* felt you encroached on my responsibility for planning the liturgies. *I* felt imposed upon and outnumbered by the staff. *I* felt cornered and didn't have a chance."

Mark does not blame Kristen for what she did to him. He refrains from using statements such as "you made me feel. . ." or "you always do. . . ." If he used that approach, Kristen might have become defensive and stopped listening, or she might have started an argument.

3. *State your reaction-behavior.* Mark continues, "Did you notice that since that situation, *I* haven't been able to talk freely to you, and *I* make sure *I* don't take my coffee break at the same time you do?" Or Mark may inform Kristen, "*I* will not be spending as much time practicing the songs with the children. *I* need more time to plan other events."

By using the win/win approach, those who are in conflict go through some behavior changes to protect themselves from being taken advantage of or hurt. They try to protect their own peace of mind.

In using one of these preceding two forms of win/win skills, people sometimes discover that both parties have emotions, that is, that both are involved in the conflict. This brings us to the third way of handling conflict, so that it can become a win/win situation.

You and someone else have a conflict with each other

Scenario

By the time Kristen and Mark finish speaking to the staff about their plans for Lent, both have become heated and are aware that they have a conflict with each other.

Skill

The best approach to this situation is the *SANE* approach, the steps of which are outlined as follows:

1. *Statement of problem:* Define the needs of all parties. This is very important. You cannot solve a conflict if you do not know what it is.

   Both Kristen and Mark state their individual needs. Kristen needs to develop a Lenten program for the adults of the parish. Mark's need is to be responsible for planning the themes for the Sunday liturgies during Lent.

2. *Alternative selection:* Brainstorm alternatives, weighing them in terms of consequences, and then choose what seems to fit best. Kristen could choose any of the following:

   • Plan six Wednesday evening sessions for the adults of the parish.

   • Extend these six themes into the Sunday liturgies.

   • Develop a RENEW follow-up program for Sunday liturgies and small group discussions.

   • Ask Mark for the list of chosen themes for the Sunday liturgies and develop six evening sessions according to those themes.

   Mark could choose any of the following:

   • Be responsible for choosing the themes for the Lenten Sunday liturgies.

   • Keep the RENEW experience in mind and plan inspiring liturgies based on the specific themes.

   • Share these themes with Kristen so she could develop small group sessions for the adults.

3. *Negotiation:* Decide who is going to do what and when they will do it. Both parties should be completely satisfied with the outcome.

   Kristen and Mark are concerned about developing an experience that will be spiritually uplifting for the parishioners. The RENEW program received positive reactions last year. Both agree it would be ideal to develop a program with a similar format for this year.

   Keeping the parishioners in mind, Kristen and Mark decide to make this a joint effort. They invite both of their committees to a meeting. The participants brainstorm themes for the Sunday liturgies, choosing one appropriate for discussions in small groups. Mark's committee will be responsible for planning the Sunday liturgies. Kristen's group will develop resource sheets to be used in the weekly small group sessions. She will also train the facilitators for the groups.

4. *Evaluation:* After having tried the solution for a while, go back and

see if it is working. If not, start the process over again.

Following the second small group session, Kristen and Mark, along with their committee members, meet to evaluate how the Lenten process is working. Comments from parishioners about the Masses, homilies, and hymns, along with reactions from the small group facilitators, are discussed. Kristen and Mark are both happy with the results and decide to continue the program as planned.

The win/win style is different from the compromise style because, if it is done properly, both parties are happy with the results. The SANE approach encourages them to work together in solving a common problem.

We have discussed three of the four skills in a win/win style. The fourth strategy or skill is to be used when there is no conflict between people.

No one is experiencing conflict

Scenario

Kristen and Mark certainly do not fit into this scenario. They did have a conflict. However, if a staff composed of several members is experiencing absolutely no conflict, we become suspicious and question whether staff members have invested themselves in the staff or team. We justify this question because broad experience has shown us that when a person values an idea and stands by certain principles, tensions inevitably arise among staff members. Thus, if there are no conflicts, we wonder to what degree staff members are sharing and planning with one another.

Skill

The strategy to be used at such times is one that encourages creativity and growth. When we encounter a staff that has no conflicts, we encourage them to share both personal and group concerns on a deeper level and to think up new ways of interacting.

Just because an individual is willing to risk managing conflict according to the win/win style, it does not mean that other people will be willing to take the same risk. They may refuse to enter the struggle and walk away. If this should occur, the person will have to settle for less and use one of the other methods of conflict management: win/lose, avoidance, compromise, or accommodation. We encourage staffs to do their best, and we challenge them at least to do something to help manage the conflict situation.

Having learned how to manage conflict according to a win/win style, the staff is asked to reflect on personal conflict situations once again and to ask themselves which of the four skills related to the win/win approach best fits their case. Those wishing to share insights with the group are encouraged to do so. In a spirit of respect for confidentiality, names and specific situations are withheld. We don't want to jeopardize any healing or reconciliation. The sharing of personal conflicts helps the group to reach a deeper level of trust. It also helps the group learn how to handle future conflict situations.

After the discussion on conflict management, we ask the staff to look closely at one of the major causes of conflict, burnout. Conflicts don't always occur between people. Sometimes they take place within ourselves because of our own expectations and those of others. Unrealistic expectations can eventually lead to burnout if we are not careful.

Burnout describes the state of a person who has become exhausted with his or her profession or major life activity. Burnout occurs in all walks of life. People involved in ministry, however, are more prone to it because they are susceptible to a messiah complex, that is, they try to be the saviors. Ministers tend to say yes to everything and often forget about themselves.

In *Ministry Burnout* John Sanford lists nine reasons why people in ministry are prone to burnout. The following conflicts face the ministering person:

1. A job that is never finished.
2. Inability to determine if her or his work is having any results.
3. Involvement in repetitive work.
4. Dealing with people's expectations.
5. Working with the same people year in and year out.
6. Experiencing a drain on energy because she or he works with people in need.
7. Dealing with many people who come to her or him or the Church not for solid spiritual food, but for strokes.

8. Functioning a great deal of the time on her or his persona. The *persona* is the front or mask we assume in order to meet and relate to the outer world, especially the world of other people.

9. Becoming exhausted by failure.[9]

Ministers can go through various stages, which, if not watched closely, can lead to burnout. We describe four stages in particular, and we offer staffs responses to these stages to help them prevent burnout.

The first stage is that of *over-enthusiasm*. Individuals in ministry tend to be perfectionists and overly enthusiastic about their work. For them, the sky is the limit, and their energy never ends. They are very committed to their job, deeply motivated, and very involved. To protect oneself from over-enthusiasm (and thus over-extension), it is important to know that the ideal and the real will never meet. The ideal is what draws us forward, but we can't go beyond what is reasonable. We encourage staff members to develop a clear sense of the requirements of their job and their own expectations. No one can be all things to all people. The way to respond to perfectionism and over-enthusiasm is to function within realistic limits of time and energy. We remind staffs that individual members will make this response in unique ways.

If careful attention is not given to the possibility of burnout at this first stage, individuals enter the second stage of burnout known as *stagnation*. In this stage exhaustion takes over. A person feels stuck in a rut, and the ideal becomes elusive: it's the same old routine over and over. The person begins to question her or his abilities and role, and she or he becomes less capable of handling simple situations. Decisions are no longer easy to make and judgments are often poorly made. People in the stagnation stage need to find a support person or group to challenge them to explore reasons for doing their tasks. They should try out new, creative ways of operating. Sometimes changing environment and mode of operation helps individuals out of the stagnation stage.

If these steps are not taken, people move to the third stage, *frustration*. At this stage, people can no longer handle the routine of everyday work and have often lost all sense of creativity. They become angry and uninvolved. Their work becomes a nine-to-five job instead of a ministry. They are at a point of merely coping with life. Even physiological changes such as loss of appetitie, lack of sexual desire, and sleeplessness may take place.

Individuals experiencing frustration need professional help on three levels. Physically, they need more rest, exercise, and a better diet to maintain a better perspective on their job. Emotionally, they need psychological help to restore a sense of self-worth and meaning. Spiritually, they need direction and prayerful reflection to help them see the value of their ministry.

It is our hope that staff members on the road to burnout receive help before reaching the final stage, *apathy*. If they do not get help, individuals tend to withdraw from other people and their jobs. They think no one cares. Their negative attitude becomes very cynical. They see their friends as enemies. They experience a deep sadness leading to depression. If this situation continues, individuals run greater and greater life-threatening risks; for example, they may acquire some form of chemical dependency. The only way a person can be helped at this stage is to take a leave of absence or leave the job entirely and look for something new.

Because staff members work closely together, we suggest they show concern for each other by maintaining a careful watch for these stages of burnout. We also suggest four antidotes to prevent burnout:

1. Find a support group of persons with whom you can be yourself.
2. Work on improving self-esteem and emphasize your successes.
3. Have fun and pursue leisure interests.
4. Exercise self-discipline, especially in your use of time as a minister.

Following the presentation on stages leading to burnout, we allow time for questions. We conclude this session with a reading from St. Paul's letter to the Thessalonians, book 1, chapter 5, verses 14 to 21.

The time spent in the first four sessions gives staffs opportunities to grow closer together and provides occasions for understanding and appreciating one another better. Ideally, the level of cohesiveness that has been reached should deepen as the months and years go by. However, our research tells us that over half of the staff members on a parish staff change jobs every three or four years. With this in mind, the final session of the team-building process is designed to help staffs deal with termination.

Session 5: Termination

Focus: Evaluating work and interaction and helping staffs through transition periods.

Process: Skills for determining success and failure and setting new directions.

Agenda: Prayer
              "Beatitude of Mourning"
              Reflect on experiencing termination in a community
              Group sharing
              Evaluation of team-building process
                 History line
                 "What was most and least helpful?"
                 "What more needs to be done?"
              Wrap-up
              Closing prayer/celebration

The session on termination needs to be adapted to the individual group. One parish staff may be going through the team-building process at a time when it is not losing any members. They end these sessions by realizing their need to continue working with each other in order to deepen the interaction begun by this process. Another staff, however, may be losing members. This means saying goodbye and recognizing that new members joining the group in the coming year will create a different spirit. We present this session in varying ways, depending on the type of termination we are dealing with.

We begin the session in the spirit of gratitude for the individuals who make up the group, and read from Paul's letter to the Philippians, book 1, verses 3 to 7 and 9 to 11. We then pass out enough index cards so that individuals have one card for each staff member in the group, excluding themselves. Each person puts the name of one staff member on the top of each card. We give the staff members ten minutes to write on the cards the aspects they like about each person and how they see each person's gifts being used for the parish. Afterwards, the cards are read aloud in the large group. Members listen to what the rest of the staff has to say about them. If done in a prayerful way, this is an affirming experience. After everyone has had a chance to be affirmed, a *Glory Be* is prayed together.

Following the prayer time, if the group is losing one or more members, a selection from the "Beatitude of Mourning" from Peter Van Breemen's *Called By Name* is read in order to set the tone for this session.[10] In the selection Van Breemen speaks of the word *care* as rooted in the Greek word *kara*, which means mourning. The basic meaning of care, therefore, is to grieve, to experience sorrow, to cry out. Thus, caring suggests that a person share the sorrow of another.

As staff members prepare to leave a parish, they often grieve as for a death. However, they often find it awkward to talk to their colleagues about these feelings, and vice versa. The anxiety and frustration of letting go and looking at new possibilities arouses a variety of feelings. Departing staff members experience sadness mixed with confused joy about the future. In this session we try to facilitate a more comfortable way of handling these emotions.

The first step is to acknowledge that there is confusion. In order to provide an environment for this to take place, we summarize Sofield and Hammett's "Experiencing Termination in Community." We have found the article a valuable tool for helping people express hidden emotions related to termination.[11] The article draws on Elizabeth Kubler-Ross' classic work on death and dying as a model for an individual's experience of termination of a meaningful relationship. Kubler-Ross' five stages of dying—denial, anger, bargaining, depression, and acceptance—are also experienced when any relationship ends. Not only does the person experience the pain of the present loss, but each loss, no matter how insignificant, serves as a symbol of the unfinished grieving of intense past losses. Grieving is never completed; a present loss serves as a catalyst that brings unresolved feelings to the surface again.

Sofield and Hammett point out that people go through a series of terminations and separations, and each trauma marks a stage in the development of the individual. The process begins at birth as the child is separated from the mother's womb, and it continues as the person develops a sense of independence, separating from significant people throughout life until the ultimate separation, death. Although as Christians we profess to be resurrection people, too often that profession is more rhetoric than reality. That is, we say we are death-defiers, but we don't really believe it or act as if we believe it. And yet, it is vitally important that individuals not be passive victims of termination. To avoid such passivity, Sofield and Hammett suggest the following:

1. Attempt to isolate and identify feelings.
2. Accept each feeling as appropriate.
3. Talk about your feelings.
4. Allow any other people involved to talk about their feelings.
5. Ritualize the loss.
6. Allow yourself the time and space to grieve.
7. Reinvest yourself in new relationships and situations.

After their individual reflection, the staff members are called together and asked to share the thoughts and feelings they garnered from reading the article. We find it best not to pressure people but to allow for voluntary sharing. Emotions often run high during this session. Thus, although we make it a point to acknowledge the feelings of sadness in a group, we also encourage the group to remember that resurrection comes after passion and death. We help the group move toward a vision of new life even if it cannot be felt at the moment. The staff is encouraged to celebrate the joys they have experienced and to muster strength to move into the future.

The final step in the process is evaluation. With the help of a typed history line that briefly describes the previous team-building sessions, we ask the group to reflect on its history, focusing on the significant moments—both the ups and the downs—experienced during the team-building process. Group members receive a worksheet that includes the following questions:

1. What was most helpful to you in the team-building process?
2. How has the process affected you as a person?

3. What was least helpful to you? Why?
4. Has the group changed because of these sessions? How?
5. What is still needed to enhance the spirit of team ministry in this group?
6. Other comments.

We give the group fifteen minutes of quiet time to write their answers to the questions. Meanwhile, we draw a history line on a large sheet of newsprint and indicate on it the five sessions of the team-building process, as shown below.

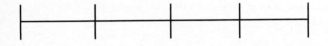

Faith   Collaboration   Variety of   Handling   Termination
Sharing   Gifts   Conflict

Staff members are asked to share their responses to the questions. As they verbalize what was most and least helpful, these comments are written on the newsprint. In most cases, areas that some found helpful, others did not find helpful at all, and vice versa. This exercise gives the group some insight into its own diversity. Thus, when the group makes plans for the future, the group will know that some methods of handling situations may not have the same appeal for all members.

On another piece of newsprint, we mark down comments on how the group feels it has changed because of the team-building process and on what the group feels still needs to be done. Once the information from the worksheet is summarized on the newsprint, we read it aloud. This gives group members a chance to listen carefully to all their achievements, to congratulate themselves on how much they have grown as a group, and to focus their efforts on the future. Some parish staffs have a clear sense of what needs to be done, while others see two or three different areas that need attention. We encourage the latter groups to choose one area to address for the next few months, rather than to try to handle a number of areas all at once.

We close this final session with a spontaneous prayer of thanksgiving, and follow it with a meal as a means of celebrating the entire team-building experience.

Some parish staffs need to go through all five sessions to become a better working group. Others have already had the opportunity of sharing some of the information provided in the sessions so the team-building process is adapted to better suit their needs. In whatever way the process is used, however, all involved must truly desire to work on team-building if the group is to move successfully in that direction. Our experience shows that the time and effort invested by dedicated members brings about significant changes in group interaction, and, in the long run, the entire parish reaps the benefits of the team-building process.

NOTES

1. Carol Wisniewski Holden, *Report of Parish Teams* (Chicago: Parish Evaluation Project, 1985).

2. Wendell L. French and Cecil H. Bell, Jr., *Organization Development*, 2d ed. (Englewood Cliffs, N.J.: Prentice Hall, 1973), p. 119.

3. The Myers-Briggs Type Indicator is a measure of personality dispositions and interests based on Jung's theory of types. This tool is available from the Parish Evaluation Project or any certified consultant. We have also relied on and recommend an adapted form, "The Keirsey Temperament Sorter," answer sheet, and scoring instructions, to be found in David Keirsey and Marilyn Bates, *Please Understand Me* (Del Mar, Calif: Prometheus Nemesis Publisher, 1978), p. 5–12. For more background on personality types, see Isabel Briggs Myers, *Introduction to Type*, 2d ed. (Gainesville, Fla.: Center for Applications of Psychological Type, 1976).

4. A list of the "Mutual Usefulness of Opposite Types" may be found in Myers, *Introduction to Type*, p. 5.

5. It is important to note that people who have a strong score in one of the functions may not be able to shift easily into another function. For more on dominant functions and on the strengths and shadows of other functions, see Isabel Briggs Myers and Peter B. Myers, *Gifts Differing* (Palo Alto, Calif.: Consulting Psychologists Press, 1980) and Keirsey and Bates, *Please Understand Me*.

6. G. Douglass Lewis, *Resolving Church Conflicts* (San Francisco: Harper & Row, 1981), p. 10–11.

7. Ibid., p. 11.

8. The four styles are discussed in Lewis, *Resolving Church Conflicts*, p. 10.

9. John A. Sanford, *Ministry Burnout* (New York: Paulist Press, 1982), p. 5–16.

10. Peter G. Van Breemen, SJ, *Called by Name* (Denville, N.J.: Dimension Books, 1976), p. 150–52.

11. Loughlan Sofield and Rosine Hammett, "Experiencing Termination in Community," *Human Development* 2, no. 2 (Summer 1981), p. 24–30.

Further Reading

Dyer, William. *Team Building—Issues and Alternatives*. Reading, Mass.: Addison-Wesley Publishers, 1977.

Flagel, Clarics. *Avoiding Burnout: Time Management for DRE's*. Dubuque: Wm. C. Brown C., 1981.

Francis, Dave, and Don Young. *Improving Work Groups: A Practical Manual for Team Building*. San Diego, Calif.: University Associates, 1979.

Lewis, G. Douglass. *Resolving Church Conflicts*. San Francisco: Harper & Row, 1981.

Keirsey, David, and Marilyn Bates. *Please Understand Me*. Del Mar, Calif.: Prometheus Nemesis Publisher, 1978.

Myers, Isabel Briggs, with Peter B. Myers, *Gifts Differing*. Palo Alto, Calif.: Consulting Psychologists Press, 1980.

Sanford, John A. *Ministry Burnout*. New York: Paulist Press, 1982.

Sofield, Loughlan, and Rosine Hammett. *Inside Christian Community*. New York: Le Jacq Publishing, 1981.

Chapter 6

PASTORAL COUNCIL: NETWORKING COMMUNITY

One of the most difficult areas of leadership in Catholic parishes is the parish council. Pastors groan as the date of the monthly council meeting approaches. Council members steel themselves for a long evening of hassling over matters about which they know little. In parishes where staff members are supposed to be present, they schedule ''pressing engagements'' for that night so they will have an excuse for not attending. Parishioners, when they see the published minutes of the meeting, wonder why on earth that group of fifteen people spent three hours trying to decide such mundane matters as printing raffle tickets, getting workers for bingo, or choosing what kind of ice cream should be served at the social.

We witnessed one parish council meeting in which the members spent forty-five minutes trying to decide how to warm up the hot dogs for the school lunch program. Volunteer cooks were putting them into tubs of hot water to save time in cooking—the same tubs the janitor used for washing out his mops. This was the critical issue for the monthly meeting of the council! Much of this anguish and confusion can be alleviated by clarifying three aspects of the council: purpose, structure, and operation.

The Purpose of the Parish Council

By purpose we mean the council's reason for existence, the role it performs, and how it is viewed by the parishioners. Although the Second Vatican Council was the impetus for the emergence of parish councils, long before they appeared, parishioners acted as advisors (trustees) to aid pastors in running the parish. But Vatican II raised the level of parishioner consultation so that all members were given the right to participate in the ministry and leadership of the parish. Vatican II declared that people had this right by reason of their baptism. No longer were they second-class citizens of the Church; all were people of God.

The 1983 Code of Canon Law reaffirms this right in Canon 536, which suggests that the bishops establish a pastoral council in each parish. This Canon also specifies that the pastoral council should be presided over by the pastor and made up of people engaged in the pastoral care of the parish. Their task is to help foster pastoral action in the parish, hence the name "pastoral council."[1]

The brief description of a pastoral council in the 1983 Code of Canon Law supports our recommendations for a good model for councils, that is, a council of ministries. Canon 536 also specifies that the pastoral council has only a consultative vote. Unfortunately, this discourages parishioners from sharing with the pastor the decision making and overall direction of the parish. In some places the council does exercise a strictly consultative voice. But in others a more nuanced interpretation of a "consultative vote" is applied. These councils rarely vote to reach decisions. Instead, they arrive at decisions by consensus, a process that includes prayer, discernment, and much discussion. The pastor and people work so well together that it is no longer a matter of the pastor consulting the council. The pastor and council work in a united effort to help the parish become more responsive to the Spirit and to the needs of the people.

Some parishes have established a shared leadership role for parish councils in which the pastor shares the role of chairperson with two others. All three people are responsible for effective and productive council meetings. The pastor and chairpersons meet ahead of time to work out the meeting's agenda, and they run the meeting together. After the meeting is over, the three compare notes to see what can be done to make the next meeting better.

The image the council should project in the parish is that of a group of dedicated people who are giving two or three years of their lives to discuss, discern, and plan programs so that the limited resources of the parish are used to best advantage. This is the ideal we hold up for pastoral councils. To clarify the roles and duties of the council, we suggest the following list of do's and don'ts:

Do

1. Discern what God wants of the parish community. *Discern* implies a unique way of making decisions and setting policies. When an important issue comes up, council members should stop to pray over the issue, trying to let go of biases and vested interests. Then they can come to a consensus on the best direction to follow—best for the parish and not necessarily the one that fits their own desires.

2. Discover the needs of the parishioners, especially of the less vocal and less active members. This can be done through surveys, random phone calls, suggestion boxes, or whatever other means will tap the pulse of the community.

3. Act as a model of Christian community and leadership to the rest of the parish. This means that council meetings must allow time for prayer, Bible reading, and sharing faith experiences.

4. Link the organizations, projects, and ministries of the parish together so that people know how their group or activity fits into the larger parish community. This linking is the primary feature of a council of ministries. People are not elected to the council from the parish at-large, but serve on the council only after spending time in an area of parish ministry.

5. Work with the pastor and staff, sharing responsibilities and duties, so that the parishioners see the leaders as working together and not as one group pitted against another. Consultation works best when pastor, staff, and council share the leadership role as a single unit and not as competing separate entities.

6. Handle crises that come up in the parish, especially ones that are too big or too "sticky" to be handled by other groups. These might include matters in which a large expenditure of funds is required, or issues affecting the spiritual well-being of the parish. Too often the pastor bears the brunt of these crises. If the council can work with the pastor in these difficult situations, then the crises become moments of opportunity rather than disaster.

7. Convene periodic, parishwide meetings so that all parishioners have a chance to experience firsthand the activities and projects of parish groups, as well as to air grievances. These periodic gatherings of the entire parish can be important occasions for community building, feedback, and evaluation. However, if people are going to come away from such meetings with a positive attitude about the operation and future direction of the parish, the meetings must be well planned and executed.

8. Train newly elected members of the council so that the tradition of effective consultation and policy setting is maintained. This training is a unique opportunity for peer ministry—that is, a ministry performed by those parishioners leaving the council and not by the priests or staff members.

Don't

1. Be the doers of parish activities and projects. The council is to set policy and overall direction in the parish. It then delegates to others—either commissions, committees, or organizations—the task of carrying out these policies. This is a difficult lesson for councils to learn. The temptation is to get entangled in the details of planning and ministering, instead of leaving them to other parish groups and committees. Council members might be involved in another parish ministry, but as council members, they should be free to provide guidelines and a framework for action. Letting go of control is a ministry in itself.

2. Be an in-group so that parishioners consider the council a closed, self-contained clique that has control of the purse strings and runs the parish with no outside accountability or control. We recently came across a council that, by majority vote, fired the director of religious education in the parish. The pastor was not happy with this, but did not want to cause more division by vetoing the council's decision. This is an unfortunate use of power and authority. Just as the pastor can misuse his authority, so can the council. The council is to be of service to the pastor, staff, and parishioners. Once that understanding is lost, the council no longer is operating within its legitimate jurisdiction.

3. Be a rubber stamp so that whatever the pastor or staff members want gets approved by the council. Instead, an atmosphere of mutual trust and accountability must be established so that pastor, staff, and council respect each other's opinions and contributions to the decision-making process of the parish. Some parish councils are a collection of people involved in various parish organizations and programs. They meet once a month to inform the pastor and other parish leaders of their group activities and to solve such conflicts as who will get to use meeting rooms for the coming month. Eventually this model of council becomes an exercise in report giving and calendar planning, with little input related to parish policy or priorities. Such a council, while helpful in furthering communication, falls short of the consultative role described previously.

4. Split into factions. Although council members should represent various ministries in the parish, this representation must not be controlling or divisive. Members are to consider what is best for the parish as a whole rather than what is best only for liturgy, education, or social service areas.

This list of do's and don'ts provides a general guideline for defining council roles and duties. Every council must periodically make up its own statement of purpose and list of duties—at least every four years. The constant turnover of membership produces a lack of continuity that can lead to confusion and apathy if such updating does not take place.

A statement of purpose is not that difficult to formulate. With preparation and direction, a statement can be drawn up in an evening's meeting. The process might follow the steps listed below.

1. Before the meeting takes place, council members prepare themselves by reading over materials provided by the leaders, such as sample purpose statements, roles and functions, and do's and don'ts for parish councils.

2. The leaders arrange the meeting room to create a prayerful atmosphere, removing tables and putting chairs in a circle. Each council member is asked to bring a Bible to the meeting and to be ready to spend three hours discerning the purpose or "mission" of the council.

3. The meeting begins with meditative music and a reading from Scripture that centers on the theme of discipleship, community building, or leadership.

4. After the reading everyone is directed to find a quiet place in the building or outside, weather permitting. Using their Bibles, the members are asked to look for a passage they feel describes the role or function of the council. The leaders may invite people to choose a particular passage or to open the Bible at random to see what that might produce.

5. After fifteen minutes of individual reflection, council members return to the large group. Each person is asked to share briefly the theme of the passage he or she found, perhaps quoting a verse or two and indicating what it meant to them. There should be no discussion at this point, only prayerful sharing.

6. After all have had a chance to share their passage, the leaders ask the group for insights into common themes or important emphases, key ideas, or phrases. A summary of these insights is listed on a chalk board or large piece of newsprint for all to see.

7. Once this list is complete, each council member is given an index card. Each member is then asked to look over the list

on the board or newsprint, to reflect on his or her previous reading, and then to write on the card a statement of the council's purpose.

8. Depending on the number of people present, the leaders divide the council members into groups of four or five persons, ask for volunteers to serve as small group leaders, and then invite each group to participate in an exercise of active, creative listening. One at a time, each person reads aloud his or her statement to the small group while everyone else in the group listens intently without comment.

9. After every member has read his or her own statement, the small group leaders ask people to identify common phrases or statements that can be used as a basis for one group statement.

10. Using the best ideas, phrases, and insights from individual statements, each small group constructs a single statement, one that all participants can accept, own, and feel good about presenting to the entire council.

11. The purpose statements from each small group are brought back to the large gathering. All council members listen without comment to each small group's statement. Once all the small group statements are read, the council leaders ask everyone to spend a moment in quiet prayer to ask for God's help in discerning the best aspects of each statement.

12. After a period of silent prayer, the group statements are read again, and everyone is asked to look for common themes, phrases, and ideas in order to combine the statements into a single statement of purpose acceptable to all present.
(Note: It may be possible to formulate the single statement at this time. The more common experience, however, is that the final wording will have to be worked out by a special committee made up of one person from each small group.)

13. Once the group or a special committee has drawn up the final version, the council approves and ratifies the statement. The ratification can take the form of a prayer service in which the statement is divided into sections. One or two council members read a section out loud and indicate what they feel is the key word in that section and what it implies.

14. At the conclusion of these reflections, the statement is read aloud by the council in unison. Then, while an appropriate song is played, everyone comes forward and signs his or her name to the purpose statement.

One council statement produced as a result of this process reads, "St. Bartholomew's Parish Council is a faith-filled leadership body, guided by the Holy Spirit and the Gospel, that works in conjunction with the pastor and parish staff, to discern the needs of the parish and, by setting goals and priorities, guides the parish in building a Christ-centered Christian community for the honor and glory of God."

The purpose statement helps channel people's energy and attention over the year and provides a framework for future action. Once a council has a purpose statement, it can formulate a list of do's and don'ts or a set of goals that helps the council fulfill its purpose. A sample set of goals for a parish council might be worded as follows:

1. To discern future directions for the parish.
2. To review policies, budgets, and goals for parish groups to make sure they reflect the overall purpose and direction of the parish.
3. To help solve problems brought to the council by the commissions.
4. To participate with the pastor, staff, and commissions in the decision-making process of the parish.
5. To set a good example of spiritual community in the parish.
6. To listen to the concerns and needs of the parishioners.
7. To be open and honest with one another, airing difficulties at the council meetings and not with others outside of the meetings.
8. To coordinate and link together all parish ministries and groups.
9. To communicate the goals, policies, and decisions of the council to the entire parish community.
10. To dream up new directions and to discover new avenues of growth for the parish as a whole.
11. To see to it that the commissions coordinate, develop, and

evaluate the ministries and groups for which they are responsible.

12. To encourage parishioner initiative, involvement, and decision making at all levels of parish life and operation.

13. To work toward consensus in decision making and to encourage other parish groups to do the same.

The purpose and list of goals should not be kept secret. The parish as a whole needs to know them. To be effective, the council members, goals, and operations must be visible to the parishioners. A commissioning ceremony of new council members at the weekend Masses is essential. To facilitate even greater visibility, we recommend the strategy taken by one parish, which had a "council table" one Sunday a month at the coffee and donuts gathering after the Masses. Parishioners could ask council members questions and raise issues. A large sign hung behind the table stated the council's purpose and function in the parish.

The importance of visibility cannot be stressed too strongly. Without it, a parish and a council are in trouble. For example, 50 percent of the parishioners responded "no opinion" when asked to react to the work of the parish council. Many didn't even know the parish had a council. However, in parishes where the council worked hard at being visible, that "no opinion" response fell to under 15 percent. More important, these latter parishes had little difficulty finding people willing to serve on the council.

The Council Structure

In the short history of parish councils, a number of structures have been tried. Many parish councils began as a body of selected parishioners appointed by the pastor to be his advisors on parish matters. Most of these matters related to finance or building projects. This model lasted for awhile, but then people began to challenge the favoritism associated with this approach. We recently came across a variation of this model in which each retiring council member recruited someone in the parish to replace him or her for the next term. This seemed like a good approach at first, but eventually the council became identified as a closed in-group. No amount of explanation changed this image, and the council returned to having at least half of the members elected by the parishioners.

The limitations of these models led to creating a model in which a council was elected by the parish. This model outlasted the selection approach and is still found in the majority of Catholic parishes today. However, this model is being challenged because in many cases it has become a popularity contest. Once people are elected, they often have little idea what is expected of them. Many have had little contact with parish ministries or priorities so that their advice and input are limited and their decisions poorly informed.

The Pastoral Council

The model gaining prominence today is that of the pastoral council. It is so named because that name is mentioned in the 1983 Code of Canon Law. However, it is not really clear what is meant by the term *pastoral council*. A more descriptive term would be *pastoral council of ministries*. This term implies an inherent structure in which those who serve on the council have served at least a year in a specific area of parish ministry. Only then are they nominated by their peers to serve a two-year term on the council. The following example describes how the process works.

So much is now going on in St. Jerome parish that it is more and more difficult for the priests and staff to keep in touch with all parish activities, programs, and ministries. Even the parish council itself is not able to coordinate these activities. Following the lead of the 1983 Code of Canon Law, the present council members have agreed to reorganize the council into a pastoral council, one that will coordinate and give direction to all the pastoral activities and ministries of the parish. This new council will be called a Pastoral Council of Ministries.

Articles in the parish bulletin explain this new approach. Instead of being nominated by the parish as a whole, people will run for the council from various commissions representing areas of ministry. Those who volunteer to serve on the commission will be eligible to serve on the new council of ministries. At yearly meetings all the people involved in each area of ministry will nominate three of their commission members to run for a seat on the council. The parish community will then elect one of the nominees to serve on the council for a two-year term. The pastor and one representative from the parish staff will also serve on the council.

Associated with this new council of ministries are five commissions, one for each area of ministry. The council will coordinate and link together the five areas of ministry in the parish: worship and spiritual life, education, community building, outreach, and administration. The worship and spiritual life area of ministry includes all the people who help out at the weekend Masses, as well as people involved in other aspects of spiritual life, such as prayer groups, devotions, and Lenten and Advent programs.

The ministry of education covers a wide range of services, including those related to the parish school, religious education for elementary and high school students, and adult education programs. People involved in this ministry include the school board, school faculty, volunteer religious education teachers, those involved in sacramental preparation programs, and those involved in RCIA.

The community-building ministry links together all parish organizations and groups that further the spirit of community in the parish. These include the women's club, Holy Name, senior citizens' groups, scouts, teen club, welcoming committee, sports, parish socials, dances, picnics, and breakfasts.

The ministry of outreach covers all efforts to reach out beyond the parish and its own members in order to serve the needs of the larger community. These services include ministers of care who visit hospitals, nursing homes, and shut-ins, bringing them Communion and offering companionship and care. It includes the St. Vincent de Paul Society, blood drives, the Respect For Life program, and those working on peace and justice issues.

In the ministry of administration, people serve the parish as organizers of fund-raising events, bulletin and newsletter editors, parish communication workers, collection counters, members of the finance committee, custodians of the physical plant, and planners of building projects. Finally, a sixth commission, the At-large Commission, is created so that parishioners not involved in any area of ministry in the parish will be represented on the council. This commission oversees nominations for the council, recruiting, and future planning.

Each commission will coordinate all the activities and projects associated with a specific area of ministry. Each commission will be made up of five to ten volunteers, who will serve on the commission for one year. Figure 9 diagrams the Pastoral Council of Ministries' structure.

Depending on the ministry for which it is responsible, the commission's purpose will vary. Two examples illustrate how commissions challenge, coordinate, and evaluate the groups and individuals associated with one or another area of ministry in the parish. The Worship and Spiritual Life Commission will give direction to the ministers and groups related to the Sunday Eucharist, promote the spiritual enrichment of the parish through missions, retreats, Advent and Lenten programs, and evaluate, at least once a year, the overall worship and spiritual life programs of the parish to see if they meet the needs of the people. The Community Life Commission will further a deeper sense of Christian community among all

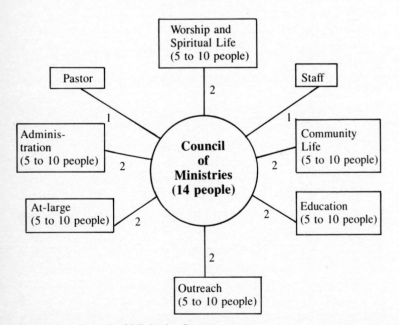

Figure 9. Council of Ministries Structure

ages and interest groups in the parish, promote ongoing communication between organizations, and sponsor periodic parish gatherings so that parishioners can enjoy a greater sense of belonging and community spirit.

At the same time that descriptions of the new council appear in the bulletin, meetings of all those involved in parish ministries are held. At these meetings a slate of nominees is prepared and presented to the parish as the first step toward the formation of the council. Some of the nominees are members of the old council, some are new faces, but all are active in one or another area of ministry.

Each person running for the council must fulfill the following criteria:

1. Be sixteen years of age or older.
2. Have served for at least two years in some area of ministry in the parish. (This criteria would change the following year to "Have served for one year on the commission they represent.")
3. Be a registered member of the parish.
4. Not be an elected officer of a major parish organization.
5. Communicate regularly with the groups and ministries the person represents on the council.
6. Live up to and accept the purpose statement and goals of the council.
7. Attend council meetings regularly. (Two consecutive unexplained absences would mean replacement by another person from the commission represented by that council member.)
8. Attend the two summer training retreats for council members.
9. Aid in the formation and continued development of the commission that person represents. (This does not mean, however, that the council members are the chairpersons or leaders of the commissions.)

Elections are held in May. In marked contrast to previous council elections, the enthusiasm among the parishioners is high. People are familiar with those running for the council from the meetings of ministers, the explanation of the Pastoral Council of Ministries in the bulletin, and from pictures of the nominees that have appeared in the parish newsletter. Even the nominees who are not elected will have a part to play because they will be serving on one of the six commissions for the coming year.

For this first election half of those elected will serve a one-year term and half a two-year term. This will provide a sense of continuity in the years to come.

Over the summer months the new council of ministries meets twice, once in a retreat emphasizing prayer and socializing and once for defining their purpose and mode of operation. The council also decides not to write up a constitution but to work out of a covenant agreement. They want to stress the faith dimensions of the council rather than its legal definition. This covenant agreement is summarized in an easy-to-read booklet that includes the council's mission statement, goals for the coming year, do's and don'ts for the council, a structure diagram, definitions of the areas of ministry for which each commission is responsible, nomination and election procedures, criteria for membership, terms of office, a checklist for delegating issues to other groups, methods for arriving at decisions, and an outline stipulating how meetings are to be conducted.[2]

A Simplified Structure for Smaller Parishes

Close to half of the Catholic parishes in the country are made up of small congregations with under five hundred members. Some of these are inner-city parishes serving predominantly black or Hispanic populations. Others are in small towns and rural areas. A council of ministries with six commissions may be too complicated a structure for a parish in these areas, although it has been used to good effect even in such smaller communities. Therefore, we would like to offer a simplified version that does away with commissions and forms a closer link between parishioners and the council.

In many small parishes the staff is made up only of the pastor and volunteers who help with the music and religious education. The council is a collection of the most active parishioners, who may belong to four or five different groups or serve in a number of parish ministries. Such a structure leaves little room for new blood. A simplified council of ministries, however, can help to create openings for more people to become involved in the running and operation of the parish.

The first step is to make a list of all the current organizations and ministries going on in the parish. Once the list is complete, add to it all the other groups or activities that are needed but have not as yet been organized. For instance, the parish might have a women's club but no men's group; it might have a teen club but nothing for young adults.

Divide the list of present and perspective activities and projects into areas of ministry. Then call a meeting for all those involved in parish ministries. Separate this large gathering of people into small groups, each group related to a different area, such as liturgy, education, or administration. This forces those involved in more than one ministry to choose the one area in which they are most interested.

From each area of ministry, four to six people are selected as candidates in a general parish election. For the first year two people are elected to represent each area of ministry, one for a two-year term and the other for a one-year term. In succeeding years only one person is elected (to serve a two-year term) for each ministry. Council members do not have a commission to report to, but instead, three or four times a year, they gather together all those serving in their area of ministry to assess needs, talk over successes and failures, and plan future events and new directions. A diagram for a simplified council of ministries is given in Figure 10.

The Council Operation

Thus far we have dealt with parish council purpose and structure. But these are not enough to assure success. The way a council operates dictates either a promising future or possible failure. Operation includes the way a council conducts its meetings, makes decisions, delegates authority, and provides for year-to-year continuity.

Our experience with parishes has shown us that most parish meetings are run poorly, but council meetings are usually run in the worst fashion. Council members assemble once a month for an evening meeting. They are tired from a full day's work and are facing another three or more hours of listening to boring reports, of

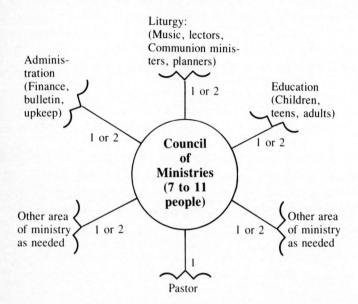

Figure 10.   Simplified Structure for Pastoral Council of Ministries

bickering over parish budgets, and of dealing with parishioner complaints. It is no fun for anyone. But it doesn't have to be that way, especially if the council is willing to let go and allow other groups and commissions to do the work.

Suppose you are a member of the parish council and it is the second Monday of the month, time for the monthly council meeting. Rather than dreading the experience, you are looking forward to it with anticipation and relish. Why? Because you know that the meeting will start and end on time. You have already received an agenda along with one-page reports from each commission. You know that the place for the meeting is warm and inviting, and it's Emma's turn to bring the refreshments. Her cheesecake is something special!

You also know that the meeting will not be all business. There will be time for prayer and sharing of stories and experiences since the last meeting. Tom is planning the ten minutes of scriptural reading and shared prayer. He is always so creative and inspiring.

The prayer will be followed by fifteen minutes of "rebonding" during which people have a chance to talk about what has been happening in their lives. Some of the council members look on this time as the most productive part of the meeting.

Next comes time for commenting on the commissions' reports. This is not a report-giving time, but a chance for people who have read the reports before the meeting to ask questions and give feedback. Then comes the business part of the meeting. This is where the council tries to delegate to the commissions and subcommittees as many agenda items as it can. The council employs the following criteria as it delegates issues and concerns to other parish groups:

1. Is the issue an important matter that the council must handle or can it be funneled to one of the commissions or subcommittees? This first criteria allows the council to let go of most of its business. If the issue is related to liturgy, then the worship commission can handle it. If it is a fund-raising matter, then it is assigned to the administration commission. If it is a problem in the school, then it is assigned to the education commission.

2. What instructions should be given to the commissions? When the council delegates issues to other groups, it does so with one or more of these requests: (a) gather the information we need so we can make a decision about it later; (b) you make the decision about this issue, for we trust you and give you our support on whatever you decide; or (c) we feel one aspect of ministry under your care needs attention, thus we are holding you accountable for determining what can be done to improve the situation.

3. Does this particular issue demand a policy statement, guidelines, or directives from the council, so that when a similar issue is raised, everyone knows what criteria to follow?

4. Is the issue important enough to be presented to the entire parish community for comments and prayerful discernment? In this way the council members realize that one of their functions is to be the discerners of the parish. This means they do not settle critically important issues without first hearing the opinions and desires of the people.

Each item on the council's agenda is measured against these

criteria. Every attempt is made to let go of as many issues as possible. There is no need to do what others can do, perhaps with greater skill and ability.

The following sample agenda items illustrate how the council follows the preceding criteria. The first item is a request from a concerned parishioner asking that the life-sized Nativity scene be set up outside of the church this coming Advent. It has been a long-standing custom in the past but has been dropped in recent years. The council, using its check-list for handling issues, decides that the Worship and Spiritual Life Commission should handle this issue and make a decision on its own. The council suggests the commission meet with the concerned parishioner, make a decision, and then inform the council of the decision through the commission representatives on the council.

The second item is a question about whether to sponsor again this year a beer garden as part of the annual carnival. In the past it has brought in a great deal of money, but some parishioners feel it is getting out of hand. They are afraid someone might drink too much and have an accident on the way home. This issue is sent to the Community Life Commission, with instructions to discuss possible options, gather information, and make recommendations to the council. The council will then establish a policy for the next carnival.

The staff representative brings a third item to the council: a discussion the staff had about working with the Parish Evaluation Project in the coming year. The council decides this is an important matter because it requires a substantial commitment of time, energy, and money. But the council needs more information from the staff about the project and from the finance committee about whether the parish can afford it. The council realizes that it needs extra time to deal with this, so the council agrees to discuss it further at a future meeting.

The fourth item is an urgent message, sent by the blood drive chairperson through the Outreach Commission representatives. The chairperson requests advertising the parish blood drive; only a very few people have signed up. The council responds by encouraging all of the commissions to seek out volunteers. The council also requests the Communication Committee to put notices in the parish bulletin and newsletter and to see to it that announcements are made at the weekend Masses.

Finally, the pastor asks the council to start thinking about how to begin the sanctuary renovation project that has been on the back burner. The council realizes that this is a very important issue and must eventually go to the entire parish for prayer and discernment. The council members begin the process by asking the Worship and Spiritual Life Commission to form a special Renovation Committee. This committee's task will be to research diocesan guidelines and draw up possible options and models for future deliberation.

These are but a few of the many agenda items that may be dropped in the laps of council members. In most cases they can respond by funneling these issues to the appropriate commissions to provide more information, to make a decision on the matter, or to evaluate present practices and procedures. The council is consequently relieved of the tedious, nitty-gritty details that make most meetings such painful experiences.

The following steps formalize the procedures for running a council meeting:

1. The executive committee (pastor and co-chairpersons) prepares the meeting's agenda and distributes copies to the entire council beforehand. The agenda includes one-page reports from each of the commissions on what has happened since the last council meeting. The agenda is also published in the parish bulletin.

2. An objective, outside observer is asked to attend the council meeting and to give feedback at the end or to interject comments whenever necessary. This observer may be a former council member or a person gifted with group interaction skills.

3. The council members assemble on the same day of the month, at the same time, and in the same place. All the parishioners know when this is happening and are invited to attend if they wish.

4. The leaders prepare the meeting room so that it is conducive for a good meeting: chairs set in a circle around a table,

extra chairs included for visitors, a warm, work-oriented setting with good lighting, and, perhaps, a smoking section.

5. Everyone shows up on time and knows that the meeting will begin and end on time.

6. The person who volunteered at the last meeting to lead prayer is ready with a prayer service (about ten minutes). The service includes music, a scriptural reading, time for sharing, and petitions for the needs of the parish and council.

7. Fifteen minutes are set aside for personal reactions and experiences people would like to share since the last council meeting. This is the rebonding, community-building time most treasured by the members. Nonmembers can share, too, if they wish, but the fifteen-minute time limit cannot be exceeded.

8. Fifteen minutes are devoted to informal comments about the commission reports and minutes from the last council meeting. This is not a report-giving time, but an opportunity for members who have read the written materials beforehand to ask questions and give feedback.

9. Agenda items for the council are then taken up in turn. These issues are those left over from the last meeting, submitted by the commissions, or raised by concerned parishioners.

10. The council deals with each agenda item, using the checklist described earlier.

   a) Is it a significant matter that the council has to handle or can it be funneled to one of the commissions or subcommittees?

   b) If the issue is sent to another group, does the council need more information, want the group to make a decision on the matter, or hold the group accountable for some aspect of ministry related to their area?

   c) Does the council need to set a policy or give overall direction to the parish on this particular matter?

   d) Is this a significant issue that must be presented to the entire parish community for prayerful discernment?

11. After all agenda items have been handled, but no later than ten minutes before the end of the meeting, a summary of the

discussion is read by the reporter, the observer gives feed-back, and members and visitors are invited to give reactions to the meeting. Once the meeting is over, people may remain for informal conversation, coffee, and refreshments.

12. The co-chairpersons and pastor meet briefly with the observer to evaluate how they conducted the meeting and to discover what improvements might be made at the next meeting.

Because the council delegates so many issues to the commissions, some parishes have decided to hold council meetings only every other month. In the intervening months commission meetings take place. In this way council members, all of whom belong to a commission as well as to the council, have to attend only one meeting a month.

Other parishes, again in an effort to reduce the number of meetings, hold a leadership night once a month. For example, on the second Monday of every month, all the commissions meet in separate rooms from seven to eight-thirty in the evening. A common prayer service is then held for all groups, followed by refreshments. From nine to ten o'clock, the council meets to handle the tasks and issues left over from the commission meetings and to set policies and establish overall parish direction. This approach allows all the commission members to interact and fosters a sense of community and sharing among parish leaders.

The way in which councils arrive at decisions is of critical importance. At present, most councils arrive at decisions by voting, a process in which the majority rules. We consider this appropriate only for issues that are not divisive or will not cause hard feelings, especially for those who lose the vote. Voting can foster a competitive approach to parish decision making. Although efficient, it does not help build trust or a sense of community in the group.

Therefore, if the council has an alternative approach to decision making, voting is used only as a means of demonstrating support and unity or as a straw vote—without any power—to assess opinions and attitudes. When opinion is strongly divided, the alternative we suggest is consensus. The following example illustrates how consensus works.

After requesting the staff to investigate the Parish Evaluation

Project (PEP), the council now has before it a report from the staff about the possibility of working with PEP the coming year. The staff representative on the council makes a report on PEP and recommends to the council that it contract with PEP for a two-year period. The council discusses the project's programs, the costs involved, and the advantages and disadvantages. The person running the meeting then asks for a straw vote to ascertain group opinion. If all the council members are in favor, then the matter is settled. But if one or more persons votes against it, then the consensus model of decision making takes over.

First, the council decides whether to continue with the discussion at this meeting, setting aside other agenda items, or to put the decision on hold for a later meeting. The council must be realistic about the amount of time required to reach a consensus. In this case the council decides to postpone other agenda items and settle the PEP question. Everyone is then asked to pause for a few moments of quiet prayer, asking God's help in discovering what the Spirit is calling the parish to do. The prayer time also helps members let go of vested interests.

After the prayer each person is asked to state briefly what his or her opinion is on the matter. As each person speaks, the others listen in silence, trying to discover areas of agreement and disagreement. Sometimes it is helpful to select one person in the group, not necessarily the chairperson, to be the discerner. This person listens to the statements of each individual and reports back to the group where the disagreement lies. Concentrating on the areas of disagreement, the group looks for alternatives and options so that everyone can eventually accept the result and feel good about the outcome.

A possible option for this decision might be to try out the PEP process for its first phase: surveying parishioners' opinions. This phase lasts six months. After that time the council can decide whether or not to continue with the second phase of PEP. Because the primary reason for opposition is cost and the first phase is only one-third of the total cost, everyone is able to accept this proposal. The decision is made as a consensus.

This discerning, consensus approach should not be used for every decision, but only for those that may cause division and bad feelings. It is an important alternative when conflicts arise. What is given up in time is gained in group solidarity and unity. But decision by consensus takes practice. Don't expect it to be successful the first few times it is tried. It needs patience, good direction, and, above all, a prayerful context.

The role of the pastor must also be clarified to ensure smooth operation of the council. The 1983 Code of Canon Law indicates that the pastor is to be the head of the council (Canon 536).[3] That does not necessarily mean he must be the chairperson. The Archdiocese of St. Paul and Minneapolis, in the 1985 revision of its *Guidelines for Pastoral Councils,* provides three models of leadership for the pastor.

MODEL A: The pastor presides over the Parish Pastoral Council by actually serving as its chairperson. Thus, the pastor is not only involved in the whole decision-making process, but also conducts the Council's meetings.

MODEL B: The pastor presides over the Parish Pastoral Council by his complete involvement in the decision-making process, but the Council elects from among its members a chairperson who conducts the meetings.

MODEL C: In those cases where the constitution of an existing Parish Pastoral Council provides for a more "democratic" model, as distinct from a "consensus" model of operation, and there are compelling reasons not to change the constitution at the present time, the pastor exercises his presiding role by retaining, and exercising where necessary, the power of veto. It is presupposed that he is also involved in the whole decision-making process.[4]

The guidelines also specify that "model 'B' is to be recommended as the preferred model. It expresses better the underlying theological principle of collegiality, that is, representative members of the parish forming one body with the pastor in caring for responsibility for the life and ministry of the parish. The election of a chairperson stands as a visible sign of shared responsibility."[5]

Whether or not the pastor takes an active role in running council meetings, he is still exercising a leadership role by his presence, style, and interaction with other council members. It is possible for a pastor to act as co-chairperson with two other council members, so that in a given meeting different agenda items are led by one of the three leaders. Or the pastor might run one out of three council meetings as a model to the others of how to conduct a prayerful, efficient meeting.

Whichever approach is used, the three leaders meet afterwards, perhaps with an observer, to see what worked well, what failed, and how to improve the next meeting of the council.

NOTES

1. The Canon Law Society of Great Britain and Ireland, *The Code of Canon Law in English Translation* (London: Collins, 1983), p. 97.
2. Our Lady of Perpetual Help Parish in Hammond, Indiana, constructed a booklet of this type for its pastoral council of ministries. It is called *Parish Leadership* and can be obtained from Our Lady of Perpetual Help Parish, 7132 Arizona Avenue, Hammond, IN 46323.
3. The Canon Law Society, *The Code of Canon Law,* p. 97.
4. Archdiocese of St. Paul and Minneapolis, *Guidelines for Parish Pastoral Councils,* rev. ed. (St. Paul, Minn.: Office of Pastoral Planning, 1985), p. 6.
5. Ibid.

Further Reading

Bradford, Leland. *Making Meetings Work.* La Jolla, Calif.: University Associates, 1976.

Doohan, Leonard. *The Lay-Centered Church: Theology and Spirituality.* Minneapolis: Winston Press, 1984.

McKinney, Mary Benet, OSB, D.Min. *Sharing Wisdom: A Process for Group Decision Making.* Allen, Tex.: Tabor Publishing, 1986.

Rademacher, William J. *The Practical Guide for Parish Councils.* Mystic, Conn.: Twenty-third Publications, 1979.

Sweetser, Thomas. *Successful Parishes: How They Meet the Challenge of Change.* Minneapolis: Winston Press, 1983.

Chapter 7

MINISTRIES: MAKING THE PARISH WORK

A successful parish is one in which all levels and areas of ministry are coordinated and well directed. It is up to the commissions to make sure this happens. Chapter 6 suggested six commissions, although each parish, because of its size, people, and location, will discover what number and types of commissions fit them best.

Commissions are made up of people already active in some area of ministry in the parish. Through an annual gathering of these ministers, commission members either volunteer or are elected by their peers (that is, by their co-ministers) to serve one or two years on the commission. The ideal size of a commission is from five to twelve members. Each commission should include at least one staff person who acts as a resource, catalyst, and sounding board for commission members.

The Worship and Spiritual Life Commission, for example, might have a lector, a eucharistic minister, a liturgy planner, a choir member, an usher, and one or two members of a parish's RENEW groups. The associate pastor, choir director, or liturgy coordinator might serve as the staff resource person to the commission.

The role and responsibilities of the commissions can be summarized in the following list of do's and don'ts:

Do

1. Meet periodically with the ministers your commission represents. The Community Life Commission, for example, might

sponsor a gathering of all parish organizations twice a year in order to further a spirit of community in the parish. This gathering could include the Holy Name Society, Knights of Columbus, women's club, Scouts, teen club, senior citizens and divorced/separated groups. The Administration Commission, on the other hand, could meet periodically with its own group of ministers, including all those who do fund-raising, maintenance, communication, and budgeting in the parish.

2. Solve problems associated with your area of ministry. If, for example, the school and religious education programs for public school children are having difficulty sharing meeting rooms and materials with each other, then it is up to the Education Commission to mediate and solve the dispute in a way that builds community between the two groups. If the food pantry can't keep up with the demand for food and clothing, it is up to the Outreach Commission to rally support and increase contributions by bringing this difficulty to the attention of the parish community. If the commissions can handle conflicts, the council and staff are free to deal with larger issues.

3. Coordinate and link all groups and programs associated with your area of ministry. The Education Commission links the parish school with the other educational programs, so that it is not a separate, isolated entity of the parish. The Outreach Commission links all individuals and groups who minister beyond the parish, reaching out to the larger community, neighborhood, and world concerns.

4. Take risks in dreaming up new avenues of growth in ministry. The commission's task is to keep challenging its members and others to try out new programs, seek out new ways of operating, uncover new responses to problems. Many exciting approaches have been incorporated into parish life because people were willing to try out new ideas. This experimenting is most effective at the commission level.

5. Remain flexible so that when an individual or group brings up

a suggestion or desire, the commission's response is not "we have tried it before and it didn't work" or "sorry, that's not in our present five-year plan." For example, if one of the outreach ministers wants to start up a Social Action Committee or a lector wants to hold practices for the readers, the commissions should support and encourage such initiative. But the commissions should also test the proposals against the goals and purposes of the parish or against the particular commission's own goals.

6. Create vacuums so that there is always room for new blood and fresh faces. This is one reason why membership on the commissions should be constantly changing: it allows more people to gain practice in the ministry of coordination and integration of parish groups and saves others from becoming overextended. The commission members should create openings in the ministry for which they are responsible so that more parishioners can become involved in parish activities and functions. One of the primary tasks of the At-large Commission is to scour the parish membership lists, looking for new people to fill available positions of leadership and ministry. But all the other commissions are also responsible for opening up new positions of ministry as well.

Don't

1. Give up too quickly. You are trying to establish a new way of organizing a parish. It won't take hold immediately. Some commissions will have more success getting started than others. Use the successful ones as the models for others. Try to succeed at easier tasks to build up confidence. A parishwide ministry fair is generally a good place to start. For when people come together to celebrate, support, and learn about one another's ministry and involvement in the parish, success is almost guaranteed. Keep commission tasks concrete and realizable. Only then will it be possible to define the goals and future direction of your commission.

2. Act independently of other groups or areas of ministry. It is the council's role to link the commissions together. Nevertheless, it is also up to the commissions to work in harmony with each other and with all aspects of parish life. It makes sense, for example, for the Worship and Spiritual Life and the Education Commissions to work together on such projects as Sacrament Preparation or an Advent or Lenten series. Likewise, the Finance Committee of the Administration Commission must work closely with all other areas when the yearly budget is prepared. So, too, the At-large Commission can be a resource to the Community Life Commission in funneling new members into parish organizations and clubs. If one commission starts setting up its own kingdom, then the entire structure falls from the strain this creates.

3. Take on too much. It is up to the commissions to coordinate each area of ministry, but not to do all the work. That is up to the subcommittees to handle. The Worship and Spiritual Life Commission should make sure all aspects of the weekend Masses work toward the common goal of providing a prayerful, uplifting, celebrative experience of worship for the parishioners. But it is not up to this commission itself to plan liturgies, select the music, or find volunteers to bring up the gifts during Mass.

These do's and don'ts are put into operation by the way the commissions run their meetings. As mentioned in the previous chapter, these meetings do not have to be often, perhaps no more than once every other month. Nor need they be long in duration. The format used for council meetings applies to commission meetings as well. An agenda is prepared beforehand by the co-chairpersons and staff resource person for the commission. All members are contacted personally to remind them of the meeting and to inform them of the agenda. The chairpersons come early to prepare the meeting room so that the environment is conducive for a good meeting. This includes a warm, work-oriented setting with good lighting, chairs in a circle around a table, and a smoking section if needed. Everyone shows up on time and knows the meeting will end on time.

The person leading the meeting reviews the agenda so that everyone knows what will be discussed. The person whose turn it is to lead prayer is ready with a short service that might include a reading, petitions, and quiet reflection. A few minutes are set aside for sharing personal experiences participants have had since the last meeting. This sharing helps build a sense of community and keeps the meeting from becoming business oriented. But the personal sharing time is limited so that it doesn't take up the entire meeting.

A few minutes are used for reminding participants what was decided at the last meeting, what has happened since that time, and the general state of the commission's area of ministry. This overview should not take more than ten minutes.

The business items are then taken up in turn, according to the following progression:

1. Information items are treated briefly. They are mentioned so that everyone on the commission is kept informed about current events and can communicate the information to other groups of ministers.
2. Decision items have already been discussed at previous meetings, but must be decided on now. If people have had time to think and pray over these matters, the decisions can be made more easily. There is no need for parliamentary procedure or formal voting. Decisions are reached by consensus so that everyone can accept and live with the results.
3. Feedback items consist of responses on the strengths and weaknesses of programs or situations within the scope of the commission's work.
4. Planning items need preparation and thought. No decisions are made at this time. But people begin to make plans and start thinking about them. Evaluation of plans and information gathering are also included in this category.
5. New business includes items that have arisen since the agenda was made up or that individuals want to bring to the attention of the group. These matters can be voiced and then put on the agenda for the next meeting so that they don't take up too much time at the end of the meeting.

After the preceeding items have been handled, but no later than five minutes before the end of the meeting, people are given a chance to give feedback on how the meeting went. This is the time to talk about the process of the meeting, not about any of the items of business. This reflection time provides an essential sense of closure, and it also helps improve communication for the next meeting. The meeting adjourns on time. Informal conversation, along with coffee and refreshments, follows.

Commissions

One issue common to all commissions is membership. We suggested earlier that one or more staff persons act as resources to the group. The staff members should not be in charge of the commission, but should be the facilitators, challengers, information sources, and supporters of the group. The rest of the commission is made up of people actively involved in the area of ministry represented by the commission. The ideal size of the commission is from five to twelve people. Not all areas of a particular ministry need to be represented on the commission itself, but those who do serve on it must have a grasp of all areas of ministry coordinated by the commission. For instance, the Worship and Spiritual Life Commission does not have to have one member from the choir, folk group, ushers, lectors, servers and so forth. But the members of this commission must know the role and function of each one of these forms of liturgical ministry.

The way in which ministers become members will vary with each commission. For example, the Worship and Spiritual Life Commission may hold an annual gathering of all ministers and leaders involved in the weekend Masses or prayer/devotional groups of the parish. At this gathering people volunteer to serve for at least one year on the commission. These volunteers commit themselves to perhaps eight meetings a year. They accept responsibility for providing the overall direction of worship and spiritual life in the parish.

The Community Life Commission, on the other hand, might ask each parish organization to select one of its members to serve for a year on the coordinating commission. In this way the commission itself would be a community-building example to other groups. Its membership, therefore, might include a senior citizen, a teenager, and a representative from the singles group, the divorced/separated group, the women's club, and the Holy Name Society. The Education Commission draws its membership from the school board, the Religious Education Committee, RCIA, and the adult religious education group. The Administration Commission would be composed of representatives of the Finance, Maintenance, and Communication Committees. The Outreach Commission might hold a meeting of all those involved in pastoral care, the food pantry, social awareness, ecumenical dialogue, and refugee work. From this number a few people commit themselves to serve on the commission in order to coordinate these activities. Each area of ministry thus serves the parish with a unified purpose and direction.

Membership in the At-large Commission is unique. Because this commission represents the entire parish and not just those associated with an area of ministry, any parishioner can volunteer to serve on this commission. The role and function of the commission is to recruit new people for ministry and leadership and to aid the council and staff in overall planning and goal setting for the parish. The members of this commission, therefore, should be gifted in thinking up creative ways of contacting and encouraging parishioners to become more active in parish life and skilled in planning and goal-setting techniques. Often people who have these abilities are already active in other ministries. Once they discover, however, that they might be of better service to the parish in this area, they may switch to the At-large Commission. This allows others to take over their previous positions in other ministries.

The length of membership on the commissions varies. The minimum tenure should be one year, because it takes that long to learn the role and function of commission work. People often continue after the first year because they see the value of this coordinating ministry. But a limit, perhaps three years, should be put on their term of office. This limited tenure gives others the opportunity to use their unique talents and gifts in this leadership role.

The criteria for membership proposed in Chapter 6 indicated that only those who had served for at least one year on one of the commissions were eligible to run for the pastoral council. This might limit the field of candidates too much. Some provision can be made so that not only those who are on the commission are eligible, but also those who have served for at least two years in one of the ministries or subcommittees associated with the commissions. The list of nominees would then go to the At-large Commission for screening and final selection.

Worship and Spiritual Life

In a typical parish three-fourths of the registered parishioners attend Mass at least every other week. Less than 40 percent participate in other parish activities, however. In other words, the weekend Masses are not only the primary, but also the sole form of participation for most parishioners. For this reason the ministries associated with worship and spiritual life are of essential importance.

Unfortunately, the liturgical life of many parishes leaves much to be desired. Too often everything is reduced to the same common denominator. Each Mass becomes the same progression of songs, responses, and prayers from the missalette. No attempt is made to adapt liturgies to the needs of different groups, ages, or expectations. The parish settles into a routine that people grow to expect but do not celebrate. Each group of liturgical ministers performs its job, working independently of others, following its own schedule and mode of operation. So much is lost in terms of creativity, initiative, and inspiration.

But gather these ministers together and give them the opportunity to relate their experiences and observations about the weekend liturgies, encourage them to brainstorm ideas for improving the Masses to suit changing clientele, challenge them to perform their ministry better, link them together in a corporate effort at providing parishioners with a good occasion for worship, require from them periodic self-evaluation of their work, and the weekend liturgies take on a new tone and character. Such is the work of the Worship and Spiritual Life Commission.

Of course, much depends on the priest who presides at Mass. He greatly influences the tone and climate for worship. For this reason, all Sunday presiders should be included in these periodic gatherings of liturgical ministers. The presiders should attend as the co-workers of the other ministers and not as the authorities or experts. All liturgical ministers must work together to create a conducive atmosphere for prayer and sharing faith at all the Masses. (For information on how to help the Worship and Spiritual Life Commission evaluate the parish Sunday liturgies, see the appendix, "A Checklist for Weekend Liturgies.")

In addition to its responsibility for the weekend Masses, the commission oversees the entire spiritual life of the parish, which includes retreats, days of recollection, prayer groups, and Lenten and Advent programs of devotion and spiritual enrichment. Such activities attract smaller groups than the weekend Masses, but they are important for the continued growth and development of the more active members of the parish. These activities also provide opportunities for those who may not be active in parish organizations, but occasionally feel a need for greater faith and spiritual enrichment. The commission should foster such opportunities and coordinate the energies of parish ministers so that these programs are well developed and productive.

Community Life

This area of ministry is often overlooked in parishes. Although a parish may have many organizations, such as the women's club, Holy Name Society, scouts, and senior citizens' groups, they seldom are linked around the common goal of improving community spirit. Therefore, the purpose of the Community Life Commission is to promote communication between parish organizations, to coordinate activities and parish events, and to help all those involved in parish groups to work together toward a common goal. The scope of the commission includes all community-building events in the parish, such as picnics, carnivals, breakfasts, anniversaries, and socials.

Most parishes are too large to be considered a community. They are, instead, a collection of many smaller communities. Some of these parish subcommunities are formally established as clubs or organizations with officers, bylaws, and regular meetings. Others are more informal in makeup, such as the daily Mass-goers, the weekly coffee klatch, or the Saturday volleyball players. Few of the people involved in these groups feel they help foster community spirit in the parish. But if they are made aware of how they fit into the larger scope and purpose of the parish community, they will begin to realize what an important contribution they make to the parish as a whole. It is up to the Community Life Commission to heighten people's awareness and to form a network that links parish groups together.

Twice a year the commission can gather all the leaders (ministers) of organizations and groups together. The leaders talk about their own group and learn about others. This is also the time for filling in the calendar for the coming months, so as to avoid conflicts and overlapping events. Once each year the leaders decide who will serve on the commission for the coming year. They also nominate people to run for the pastoral council. The commission can also sponsor a community fair at which all groups and organizations display their "wares" for the whole parish to see and invite new people to join their group or recruit volunteers for their activity.

If a conflict or concern arises in connection with one of the organizations or parish socials, the Community Life Commission mediates or arbitrates the controversy, freeing the pastoral council from getting drawn into the nitty-gritty, mundane misunderstandings common to all parishes. If individuals wish to start up a new group or organization in the parish, such as a singles' group or young couples' club, the Community Life Commission helps the group get organized and guide them through the difficult formation period. The commission also screens new groups to make sure that parish organizations and activities are not multiplied beyond the capacities or resources of the parish. If other groups have served their purpose and are waning, this commission helps them through the termination stages so that they can die gracefully and with self-respect. Most parishes have no provision for termination and closure. As a result groups continue to hang on far beyond their usefulness.

The work of this commission need not be time consuming. The commission does not have to meet often, perhaps only every other month. A staff person acts as a catalyst and a support for the commission as it fulfills the subtle yet critical tasks of linking parish subcommunities together and of fostering a spirit of unity and good will among parish groups and individuals.

Education

The Education Commission coordinates all levels of educational programing in the parish, children through adults, Catholic and public school children alike. Too often a parish has a number of religious education programs, each with its own purpose, goals, and emphases. This is especially true for parishes with an elementary school. So much time and effort is required to maintain a school that little energy is left over for integrating the school's operation into a larger educational network.

The Education Commission's role is to overcome this fragmentation of efforts and to foster greater cooperation, coordination, and communication among all groups and individuals involved in the education ministry of the parish.

To fulfill this role, the Education Commission must meet the following goals:

1. To develop and continually update the purpose and focus of the entire educational effort in the parish. That purpose should be summarized in a statement that explains the general direction of the educational efforts in the parish. All groups can then use this statement as a guide for their programing and activities.

2. To encourage, support, and challenge groups and individuals involved in education to share ideas, resources, and experiences as a means of improving cooperation.

3. To ensure that all those involved in teaching or coordinating programs are trained and equipped to do their jobs well.

4. To promote the active involvement of parents in the education of their children and to ensure that all eligible parishioners are invited and encouraged to become active in the educational programs.

5. To be sensitive to the special educational needs of unique groups in the parish, such as the handicapped, minorities, or marginal members of the parish.

It is not the role of the Education Commission to do the educating or even to administer programs. Rather, the commission is to make sure that those responsible for responding to the various educational needs of the parishioners do their jobs well, that they are provided with the tools and resources necessary for their work, and that they carry out the overall purpose of religious education in the parish.

The groups associated with the Education Commission vary with each parish. For parishes with a school, these groups might include a school board, Religious Education Committee for public school children, adult education programs, and preparation programs for the first reception of sacraments. Two aspects of the education ministry need special attention because they are a source of confusion in many parishes: the parochial school and the adult education program.

The School Board

In many parishes, the school board was established before the parish council was. Its members were elected by the parishioners to advise the pastor and principal on the running and operation of the school. When parish councils were initiated, questions arose regarding the school board's position with respect to the council. In many places the school board remains a separate entity, operating independently of the council. This dual supervision structure often symbolizes a dual community in a parish: the parish community and the school community.

As a means of integrating the school community into the parish, some parishes made the school board accountable to the council, or at least allowed it representatives on the council. This was a move in the right direction, but we suggest still another step in the effort to integrate the school into the parish community. We recommend that the school board remain active as the body that aids and advises the principal in the operation of the school. But we also suggest that the board be one of a number of groups coordinated and given direction by the Education Commission. A few members from the school board might be members of the commission, but it is important that the commission have a balanced representation from all ages and aspects of the educational ministry. Otherwise, school matters and concerns will dominate the work and role of the Education Commission.

Members of the school board itself can be either volunteers or representatives elected from among a slate of nominees, all of whom are, in some way, related to the ministry of the school. The do's and don'ts for school board members are as follows:

Do

1. Set overall policies for the school, ones that reflect and manifest the overall educational policies of the parish as stipulated by the Education Commission.

2. Gather information about population changes in the area, prospective students, cost estimates, maintenance, and school expansion.

3. Work with the principal, suggesting new avenues and emphases; listen to people's special concerns and communicate them to the principal.

4. Evaluate the principal's performance, advising the Education Commission, the council, and the pastor when he or she is not performing the task well, and interview new applicants when necessary.

5. Be informed on current Catholic educational trends so as to be able to make informed judgments about school priorities and options.

Don't

1. Lose sight of the role and function of the school in the overall life and operation of the parish. Some overly protective school boards act as if the school were the only parish priority, rather than one of many.

2. Administrate the school. This is the principal's role. The board must give the person in charge of the school the room

to maneuver. The board sets policy; it doesn't implement the policies.

3. Hire or fire teachers or get involved in the evaluation or disciplining of teachers, children, or parents. Once again, this is the work of the principal. The board can tell the principal what it has heard from parents about problem areas, but it should not get entangled in the daily operation of the school itself.

The parish school is often a heated topic among parish leaders and parishioners. On one side are those who contend that a disproportionate amount of the parish budget is spent on a relatively small percentage of parishioners. For instance, 40 percent of the budget may be used for the education of 10 percent of the parish membership. The other side argues, however, that the influence of the school goes far beyond the children who attend. It affects the parents and involves them in parish activities and programs. It builds good Christian leaders for the next generation of parishioners. It sets an example for other children in the area. The intensity of the arguments on both sides of the issue grows whenever a rumor, justified or not, begins to circulate that the parish school might be closing.

The question of whether a parish should maintain a school is complex. Much depends on what other options exist: Can children receive a good religious education if the school does not exist? Are there opportunities for quality education in the surrounding area? Do the benefits of the school justify the expense? Do children who attend the school receive a better religious upbringing than those who attend the public school?

These are not easy questions to answer. A parish school in a central city location may be doing a service to Catholic, as well as to other students, because the options for good education in the area are minimal. A parish school in a suburban area may be providing an alternative structure that forms values and inculcates religious traditions that children attending religious education classes once a week might never obtain. At the same time a neighboring parish without a school may have a vibrant religious education program involving parents and volunteer teachers. It may achieve the same results as the parish that has a school. In other words, much depends on the tradition of the parish, its environment, and the leadership skills of those running the programs.

If the leaders contemplate either cutting back or eliminating the parish school entirely, they must be sure that the people are included in whatever decision is made, preferably through a process of discernment. Because people's feelings about the role of school in the parish run so deep, if a decision is made without adequate parishioner consultation, it will come back to haunt the leadership, no matter what the outcome may be.[1]

Adult Learning

Adult education is a second area that often causes confusion and frustration in parishes. When our parish surveys ask for reactions toward adult education programs, 82 percent of the people in a typical Catholic parish respond that they favor or highly favor these activities. Parish leaders invariably have been surprised by such responses, since so few show up when the parish offers such programs. That response is quite understandable, since only 4 to 8 percent of adults usually attend adult education programs.[2] Why is the attendance so low? There are many reasons: wrong day, wrong time, wrong topic, poor publicity, poor image, lack of support, and fear of being ill-equipped or unqualified.

On a few occasions, however, an adult education program meets with unexpected success. The organizers scratch their heads and say, "What happened?" While many aspects influence attendance, part of the reason is that in such cases, the leaders have used sound adult learning principles. As a means of describing these principles, we offer the following list of do's and don'ts to leaders of adult education programs:

Do

1. Create a climate that fosters the participants' self-esteem and interdependence. This includes a warm, friendly atmosphere and a spirit of openness and acceptance between presenters and participants rather than an environment of competition and one-upmanship.

2. Be explicit about your own assumptions and beliefs, what you

know and don't know, and what will be included and not included in the program. The participants must know both the contents of the program and your intentions for it. In other words, you should have no hidden agenda or implicit expectations.

3. Put the learner at the center of the process. Nothing else—the topic, presenter, or group dynamics—is as important as the participant. Provide support in the form of sponsors for newcomers, partners with whom to talk over the experience, telephone numbers of resource people, and follow-up sessions to discuss insights and answer questions.

4. Concentrate on what is important to the participants. Any factual information presented in the program is useless unless it is of value to the learners and makes a difference in their lives.

5. Use the people's experience. This is a valuable source of knowledge and needs to be incorporated into any learning situation. Encouraging people to tell their stories and relate personal experiences helps participants feel that their presence is important.

6. Facilitate the learning process by enabling the learner to become self-directed and by helping people gain meaningful new insights and experiences.

7. Help the participants to become aware of and attend to their inner learning patterns. Then design the learning processes to fit these individual patterns.

8. Be open to change, both in your own methods and presentations, and in your assumptions and expectations. Demonstrate to participants that this is a dynamic program, one that adjusts to their needs and desires rather than remains staid and inflexible.

9. Be sure people have something to show for their efforts, such as a newly acquired skill, a journal of one's learning experience, a written evaluation of progress, or a new relationship.

Don't

1. Be the experts, imparting knowledge and manipulating behavior. People are much more likely to participate if the leaders are seen as fellow learners rather than as figures of authority.

2. Use techniques as gimmicks. Nothing turns off people faster than involving them in an inauthentic process; for example, asking people to express ideas and then presenting them with the ''right'' answers is a gimmick.

3. Do all the planning and decision making yourself. Encourage the participants to take an active part in preparing and presenting the material. In this way it becomes their program rather than yours.

4. Rely on only one method of presentation. Instead, be creative in your format: use charts, games, role playing, case studies, small groups of different sizes, or anything that utilizes the varied gifts and resources of the group.

Unfortunately, most of the adult education programs offered in parishes do not actively involve the participants in the planning or decision making of the programs. Too much attention is given to dispensing knowledge. Not enough is given to helping the people discover what this knowledge has to do with their own experience. This is the primary reason that attendance for such programs is so low. Applying the above do's and dont's of adult learning to current educational programs, as well as to the Rite of Christian Initiation of Adults (RCIA), sacramental preparation classes, Bible study, and discussion sessions will do much to improve their image and increase attendance.

Outreach

The Outreach Commission coordinates the ministry related to human needs, both for parishioners and for the larger community beyond the parish. Groups associated with this commission are usually centered around two areas, pastoral care and social awareness.

Pastoral care covers activities such as the St. Vincent de Paul Society, blood drive, food pantry, visiting programs for the sick and homebound, and prayer commitments for special needs. Social awareness attacks the causes of human suffering: racism, sexism, nuclear proliferation, crime, poverty, and corporate irresponsibility. Because social awareness incorporates public policies as well as pastoral care, the Outreach Committee's involvement in this second form of ministry is more complicated than is its involvement in pastoral care. The end result, however, is the same: ministering to human needs. The Outreach Commission should foster both types of activities and make sure that they complement and reinforce each other rather than compete with each other.

The goals of the Outreach Commission are as follows:

1. To coordinate requests for temporary aid and assistance through the St. Vincent de Paul Society, food pantry, Refugee Committee, and similar groups.
2. To provide help to the homebound through a network of pastoral care.
3. To answer the people's requests for spiritual aid through a eucharistic ministers program in which volunteers visit hospitals, nursing centers, and private homes to bring Communion and to provide pastoral care to the sick and homebound.
4. To foster membership in a parishwide community of prayer that responds to special intentions and prayer needs of parishioners.
5. To foster active evangelization by sponsoring combined worship services and socials with other denominations and churches in the area.
6. To foster among parishioners an awareness that all Christians have a responsibility to recognize and to serve those in need.

7. To promote programs and institutes that emphasize respect for life, addressing the needs of people of all ages and backgrounds.
8. To participate in special events that give witness to Christian love and challenge injustice and self-seeking behavior in the neighborhood and the world.
9. To sponsor periodic service projects in the parish, such as sponsoring an annual blood drive, refugee families, or collections of food, clothing, and money for those in need.

The work of the Outreach Commission is not easy. It challenges parishioners to set aside personal concerns and priorities and attend to the needs of others. In our surveys of Catholic parishes, we have discovered that the majority of the parishioners are reluctant to become involved personally or to have the parish become involved in social issues. Only 21 percent of parishioners feel that the parish should take stands on public policy issues. Less than a third (30 percent) think that the parish should form discussion groups on such issues. Less than half (48 percent) feel that the parish should encourage people to become involved in neighborhood social action projects.

An opinion gap exists between the parishioners and parish leaders. Although 76 percent of parish staffs are receptive to a parish social action committee that would deal with issues of peace and justice, only 41 percent of the parishioners agree with the formation of such a committee. Should the institutional Catholic Church speak out on social issues? Seventy-three percent of the staffs and 52 percent of the council members say yes. But only 29 percent of the parishioners agree with this approach.[3]

Many parishioners defend their position by stating that a disjunction exists between spiritual matters and worldly concerns. They cite the American tradition of separation of church and state as the basis for their views. Staff personnel, on the other hand, cite Gospel mandates, such as the Beatitudes, as the reason a parish should participate in human rights and social justice causes. They feel that the parish and Church must take stands in defense of basic human values when these are endangered by public sentiment or behavior. These differing views on social involvement often create an impasse between the leaders and the majority of the parishioners.

Other data from our parish surveys show, however, that parishioners are willing to let the parish address individual human needs by donating money to poorer parishes, providing food and emergency shelter for the homeless, visiting the sick and homebound, helping out the unemployed and handicapped, and so on. These activities are what were once called the corporal works of mercy.

This information suggests that the way to foster parishioners' sensitivity to larger issues is to start small, with concrete acts of human caring. These activities foster an atmosphere in which people begin to feel it is all right to be concerned for those suffering alienation, hardship, affliction, and deprivation. Because people are more open to these simpler acts of human caring, the Outreach Commission will have more success if it links the two areas of pastoral care and social awareness. The first area of ministry creates a conducive environment and prepares the ground for the second.

To begin creating this environment the commission can acknowledge what people are already doing by way of care and service for others. This includes the occasional acts of kindness and concern parishioners instinctively perform for one another and for others in the larger community. Spontaneous acts, such as driving an older person to the store or to Mass, preparing a meal for a family that has experienced a death, babysitting for a friend to provide an opportunity to get away for awhile, or repairing a car or home for a neighbor, all manifest a high level of Christian service. These actions need to be recognized, encouraged, and celebrated as ways in which people carry out their vocation as Christians. Two examples of such Christian service were mentioned in the goals of the Outreach Commission: a parishwide community of prayer and a network of pastoral care.

The community of prayer is a simple approach to pastoral care, but one that results in profound power to do good. Every six months parishioners volunteer to pray fifteen minutes or more each week for the intentions of the parish and its members. Those who make this prayer commitment fill out a card that reads, ''I intend to pray _____ minutes _____ every day or _____ each week (check one) for our parish, its parishioners, staff, leaders, and ministers. I intend to do this until the next renewal period six months from now.'' The person's name and address are added to the sign-up card. These names are made visible on a special Community of Prayer board in the back of the church, hung on a prayer tree in the vestibule, or listed in the parish Community of Prayer newsletter.

We have found that in a typical parish, from two to four hundred people make this commitment every six months. At each sign-up (renewal) time, about half the people are renewing their commitment and half are new volunteers. The advantage of the community of prayer is that it requires no meetings, training, or expertise, only the time and effort to pray for fifteen minutes.

During each six-month period, a special committee keeps the community of prayer informed of special intentions and groups that need prayers. The committee publishes a newsletter each month that includes not only requests for prayers, but also responses from people giving thanks for blessings received as a result of the community of prayer effort. The parishes involved in this Christian service have mentioned the impact it has had on the life and spirit of the community as a whole; it has created an environment of loving care and service among the parishioners.[4]

The second example of Christian service is a network of pastoral care. Many parishes have introduced a volunteer program of pastoral service to the needy. Volunteers are organized around different areas of need. For example, one group of ministers takes care of the elderly and homebound; another visits hospitals and nursing homes; another provides babysitting services; still another responds to those asking for financial assistance. This last group of ministers visits those seeking aid and helps them cope with the sources of the problem rather than provides stop-gap measures. A core committee oversees the various groups of volunteers, providing training and opportunities for people to meet, talk over common experiences, and support one another.

Some parishes have fostered pastoral care by dividing the parish into smaller regions based on geographical areas. Each region consists of about one hundred families and is supervised by a coordinating individual or couple. The coordinators, in turn, recruit ten other contact people who contact ten households. The purpose is simple: to make contact with every family in the area in order to discover if they have any needs or concerns that can be addressed through the parish pastoral care programs. Initial contact is made by visiting each family in the region. During the visit the contact person gives people a parish handbook listing activities, organizations, and programs. The visitor also leaves an information sheet that asks about any special needs people might have and invites them to become involved in one or another parish activity or project. After the initial contact the regional coordinators follow up on those who have expressed an interest in becoming more involved in the parish, and they refer to the parish staff and pastoral care ministers the names of those who have requested help.[5]

These examples are but two of many ways parishes are fostering an environment of care and service. Those who become active in these projects grow more aware of underlying social concerns and areas of injustice: Why is this person out of work? Why doesn't that elderly person get enough to live on? Why is this wife abused by her husband? What can be done to get at the core issue of this person's poverty and not just deal with symptoms? These questions are the beginning of a new catechesis—instruction, through experience, about unjust systems that create alienating and hurtful situations.

Only after having such personal experience will people be able to respond to larger issues of injustice and social concern. Only then will they begin to realize the inherent connection between parish ministry and social justice. Once an environment of care and concern for concrete human needs has been established, people are more willing to address the issues of nuclear disarmament, racial or sexual oppression, and respect for human life. It is in the environment of care and concern that parishioners become able to support the formation of a parish social action committee. The task of the Outreach Commission, then, is to link pastoral areas with social awareness in a way that creates an atmosphere of care and concern for individual needs and for the larger issues of injustice and oppression in the world beyond the parish community.

Administration

The Administration Commission is responsible for coordinating the temporal affairs of the parish: how money is acquired, how it is spent, how the physical plant is maintained, and how the parishioners are kept informed about what is happening in the parish. Each of these areas is handled by a subcommittee; the Administration Commission oversees these subcommittees. The pastor or the administrator, if the parish has one, is the most likely person to act as the staff resource person on this commission.

Three committees come under the jurisdiction of this commission: fund-raising, communication, and finance. The Fund-raising Committee determines how money is obtained. Too often parish fund-raising is a conglomeration of carnivals, socials, weekly bingo, raffles, and rummage sales. Each one has its own sponsor, bank account, and organizers. Little is done to coordinate these many and varied efforts or to ascertain that they reflect a common purpose or objective.

To make sure this happens, the Fund-raising Committee of the Administration Commission has to establish criteria for fund-raisers, see to the proper scheduling of events, and make sure they are well planned and that monies raised are allocated for parish needs. The committee also brainstorms new ideas, not only for fund-raising, but also for mounting pledge drives and for increasing the Sunday collection.

One of the parishes we surveyed asked parishioners why they contributed money to the parish. Was it out of obligation, because they liked what the parish was doing, or to fund pet projects, such as the school or religious education? None of these choices was the most important. Rather, people contributed money to give thanks to God for blessings they had received. As a result of this information, the leadership decided to stress this reason in its campaign to raise contributions. The outcome was beyond anyone's expectations. The people gave as never before. The lesson to be learned from this experience is that to do its job properly, the Fund-raising Committee must gather information about people's patterns of giving, suggest options for new approaches, and offer alternatives for increasing parish income. The committee must also be in touch with parishioners' opinions about the types of fund-raisers they like and how often they should be scheduled.

The second subcommittee of the Administration Commission, the Communication Committee, works in conjunction with the Fund-raising Committee. The scope of this committee's work, however, goes far beyond publicizing fund-raisers and parish socials. Its task is to inform parishioners about parish activities and programs and to elicite from them their reactions and insights. A parish can never have too many channels of communication. Weekly bulletins, monthly newsletters and calendars, periodic mailings, and parish handbooks are tools and resources for getting information into the hands and into the consciousness of the parishioners.

So important is this ministry of communication that some parishes are not only forming a special committee whose only job is publicity and dissemination of information, but are also hiring staff personnel, either full-time or part-time, to coordinate communication in the parish. This special emphasis reaps a harvest far beyond the effort. The image and spirit of the parish increases in direct proportion to how well the parishioners are kept informed about parish events and priorities.

Communication does not flow in only one direction, however. The Communication Committee must also provide people with the means for responding to parish liturgies, activities, and programs. Such simple methods as response cards in the bulletin or a cutout reply section in the newsletter provide people with the occasion and opportunity to voice their opinions about various aspects of parish life.

Some parishes provide parishioners with a ''voice from the pew'' sheet kept in the rear of church. Every two months it stresses a different aspect of the parish, asking questions about performance, expectations, and options for the future. People are free to fill out these sheets and either drop them in the collection basket or put them in the suggestion boxes at the doors of the church. Not many people respond, but those who do provide important information about parish life and operation. The Communication Committee funnels these suggestions to the appropriate group or area of ministry for study and implementation.

The third subcommittee of the Administration Commission is the Finance Committee. Canon 537 of the 1983 Code of Canon Law states that ''each parish is to have a finance council. . . [to] aid the pastor in the administration of parish goods. . . . ''[6] This requirement is worded more strongly in the code than is the requirement to have a pastoral council. This is a sound requirement because money is not an easy commodity to manage. Wise counsel and prayerful deliberation are essential in order to avoid the pitfalls of poor investments and bad management.

A Finance Committee working independently of other groups in the parish presents a great danger, however. In many parishes the budget constructed by the finance committee establishes the priorities of the parish. The emphasis should be reversed. The priorities of the parish should be reflected in how its money is spent. Pastoral and spiritual concerns should be established first, and then the budget drawn up, not the other way around. For this reason, the Finance Committee must act as a resource and information tool for the pastoral council. The ideal interaction between the Finance Committee and the pastoral council might resemble that depicted in the following example.

At its January meeting the Pastoral Council of Ministries, with the help of the At-large or Planning Commission and after consultation with all areas of ministry, establishes a list of priorities for the coming year. These priorities are given to the Finance Committee so it can make up a budget for the new year. Members of the Finance Committee go to all six commissions to find out the funds they need for the coming year. With these figures in hand, and using the priorities list as a guide, the committee makes up a tentative budget. This is reviewed by the Administration Commission and sent to the pastoral council for approval.

The council does not get involved in the details of the budget. It examines the budget's general outline to determine if it reflects the overall goals and policies of the parish. If not, the council sends it back to the Finance Committee for revision. Once the council approves the budget, the Finance Committee notifies all areas of ministry that they can begin salary negotiations with paid personnel for the coming year. The Finance Committee also publishes the new budget as an insert in the parish bulletin.

This interplay between the council and the Finance Committee helps a parish run smoothly. The Administration Commission acts as a buffer between both groups, saving the council from added work and the Finance Committee from losing sight of the larger perspective.

Through its three committees, the Administration Commission should strive to achieve the following goals:

1. To assist the Finance Committee in consulting with the pastor, staff, and other commissions regarding expenditures and preparation of budgets.
2. To review the maintenance of existing properties and to make recommendations for the purchase or construction of additional properties.
3. To promote ongoing, two-way communication (via the Communication Committee) between parish groups and between parish leaders and parishioners.
4. To oversee the work of the Fund-raising Committee in the coordination, direction, and scheduling of fund-raising events and special appeals for financial contributions.

The work of the Administration Commission and its committees is a ministry to the same extent as is worship, education, or any of the other parish ministries. Those who are active in the administrative area must continually keep in mind this ministerial emphasis so that administration does not take on a primarily managerial connotation in which financial gains and fiscal priorities become more important than conversion or spiritual growth. This is why a close relationship between this commission and the Pastoral Council of Ministries is essential for the life and development of a successful parish.[7]

At-large Commission

The last of the six commissions may be called by a variety of names. Some parishes call it the At-large Commission, because it represents all those parishioners not involved in any group or organization and its members are not drawn from a specific area of parish ministry. Others call it the Planning or Futuring Commission, because one of its primary tasks is to help the council, staff, and other leaders set directions and make plans for the future life of the parish. Still others call it the Recruiting Commission, because it is responsible for finding new leaders and ministers to freshen the ranks of parish volunteers.

Whatever its name, the commission's function is crucial to the successful operation of a modern parish. Too often, the tasks of this commission are given to other groups to handle, along with many other duties. Eventually the burden becomes too great. As a result, some crucially important tasks don't get accomplished: long-range planning, recruitment, and providing resources. The following example illustrates how the At-large Commission might accomplish these tasks.

At the start of each academic year, a plea goes out for volunteers to become part of this commission. The commitment is for at least one year and at most two. Any adult parishioner is eligible. The qualifications for the job include imagination, dedication, and experience in planning, goal setting, evaluation, and volunteer recruitment. If someone already active in another group volunteers, the individual is asked to take a leave from that ministry for the time he or she is part of this commission.

Once the commission is formed, it has three functions to perform: screening, recruitment, and planning. The first function is of short duration. When the time comes for council elections, this commission acts as the screening committee for nominees to the council. Each area of ministry submits to the At-large Commission the names of people nominated to run for the council representing that ministry. The At-large Commission contacts the nominees and makes sure they are willing to run and that they fulfill the criteria for council members. (See the "Council Structure" section in Chapter 6 for the list of criteria for council members.)

The commission then makes available to the parish the background information on the nominees. It takes care of election details as well as a commissioning service at the weekend Masses for new council members. This commission nominates several of its own members for the council. These at-large nominees follow the same election procedures as do nominees from other areas of ministries in the parish.

The second responsibility of the At-large Commission is to recruit new leaders and ministers from the parish membership. In a typical Catholic parish, less than 20 percent of the registered parishioners attend parish functions (outside of the weekend Masses) once a month or more often. When asked why they are not more involved, about half the people say that the primary reason is that they are too busy or are not interested. But a significant percentage—close to one-third—give as the primary reason that they have never been asked, that they don't feel welcomed into parish groups, or that they don't feel qualified to attend.

The At-large Commission should seek out those people open to greater involvement who need personal contact and support to allay fears and misconceptions. This recruitment task can be accomplished in a number of ways. First, a periodic census and updating of parish files, which provides parish leaders with accurate information, should be put into a computer system so that names of parishioners can be easily accessed for special mailings asking for volunteers in various ministries and programs. Second, a "Time and Talent Sign-up Sunday" should be conducted yearly by the At-large Commission and its results funneled to other commissions for follow-up. Third, the At-large Commission, in conjunction with the Outreach Commission, should oversee a welcoming committee that reaches out to newcomers, making sure they are visited or provided with sponsors for the first few months of membership in the parish.[8]

The At-large Commission functions as the eyes and ears of the parish, always seeking people who might be future leaders and ministers. Its responsibility is to continually freshen the ranks of parish volunteers so that the same, few, faithful workers do not get overextended and give up ministering because of exhaustion and burnout.

The final sphere of responsibility for the At-large Commission is planning. This may be talked about during staff, council, or commission meetings, but unless one group is given the task of creating the environment and impetus for long-range planning, the topic is only talked about. The At-large Commission should provide other parish groups with the resources and procedures for continual, effective, and realizable planning in the parish.

For example, the Pastoral Council of Ministries, at its summer meeting, decides that, for the coming year the entire parish, in its myriad forms and functions, will revolve around the theme, "Learning How to Pray." The At-large Commission is given the task of incorporating this theme into the overall planning of the parish. In September and October the commission members write up a process sheet for the other commissions. This sheet serves as a resource to help each area of ministry reflect on how the theme of learning how to pray can be incorporated into its own programs, liturgies, and activities. As a result of this reflection process, the Worship and Spiritual Life Commission decides, among other things, to emphasize music as one way to pray. It works at improving congregational singing during the weekend Masses. The Education Commission prepares two adult series on methods and approaches to prayer for Advent and Lent. The Community Life Commission devises a number of options for prayer services during meetings and parish get-togethers. The Outreach Commission helps groups link prayer and service projects together, demonstrating the need to put prayer into action and action into prayer. The Administration Commission gathers all those involved in maintenance, finances, and communication for a special overnight retreat that emphasizes administration as a ministry and stresses the need for a prayerful rather than a business-minded approach to parish operation and structures. The At-large Commission also asks all other commissions to submit a list of short-range goals that show the ways they will reflect the overall theme of learning how to pray during the coming year.

But goals and action plans are not enough. Good planning is grounded in evaluation. "Where are we going?" and "How do we get there?" must be followed by "How close did we come?" Because the At-large Commission is aware of this, during April and May the commission asks each area of ministry for feedback about what was or was not accomplished during the year. Did the parish community learn how to pray better, both collectively and individually? What was done and what is left undone for the coming year? The At-large Commission asks all areas of ministry to brainstorm ideas either for repeating the same theme with a fresh approach in the coming year or for a new theme. In June the At-Large Commission gathers the evaluations and suggestions together and makes a report at the summer meeting of the pastoral council. The council likes the progress that has been made and decides to build on last year's theme with a new one, "Taking Ministry to Work and Home."

The At-large Commission takes this new theme and works on it. It prepares the means to implement the new theme in the life and ministries of the parish. This is how the rhythm and cycle of planning, helped by the At-large Commission, continues in the parish.

Because of its three tasks of screening nominees, recruiting, and planning, the At-large Commission plays an essential role in the life of a successful parish. These tasks can be done by other groups, but if a permanent commission is given these responsibilities, a tradition of good planning and recruiting is established and maintained. Others are then freed to concentrate on their own unique ministry and contribution to the parish community.

NOTES

1. For a description of the discernment process in parish decision making, see Thomas Sweetser, *Successful Parishes: How They Meet the Challenge of Change* (Minneapolis: Winston Press, 1983), p. 211–15.
2. Parish Evaluation Project, *A Survey of Parish Attitudes and Practices,* Rev. Ed. (Chicago: Parish Evaluation Project, 1985), p. 8.
3. Ibid., p. 2, 3, 7.
4. St. Bartholomew's Parish in Chicago, Illinois, has used a program similar to the community of prayer. This parish has called it a prayer pact.
5. Our Lady of Perpetual Help Parish in Hammond, Indiana, has developed a network-of-care ministry based on geographical regions and contact volunteers in each area.
6. The Canon Law Society of Great Britain and Ireland, *The Code of Canon Law in English Translation* (London: Collins, 1983), p. 97.
7. For additional material on the spiritual aspect of administration, see Rev. John R. Gilbert, "Parish Administration as Ministry," in *Gathering God's People,* ed. J. Stephen O'Brien (Huntington, Ind.: Our Sunday Visitor, 1982), p. 214–24.
8. The Church of Christ the King in Minneapolis, Minnesota, has devised a program to welcome newcomers based on the model of the RCIA. See Richard Moudry and Laverne Hudalla, "A Better Way to Say Hello," *Today's Parish* 16 (October 1984), p. 23–25.

Further Reading

Anderson, William. *Journeying through the RCIA.* Dubuque: Wm. C. Brown Company, 1983.

Bannon, William J. and Suzanna Donovan, S.C. *Volunteers and Ministry.* New York: Paulist Press, 1983.

Dunning, James B. *Ministries: Sharing God's Gifts.* Winona, Minn.: St. Mary's Press, 1980.

Fagan, Harry. *Empowerment: Skills for Parish Social Action.* New York: Paulist Press, 1979.

Fenhagen, James. *Mutual Ministry: New Vitality for the Local Church.* New York: Seabury Press, 1977.

Fischer, Kathleen R. *Winter Grace: Spirituality for the Later Years.* New York: Paulist Press, 1985.

Harms, William C. *Who Are We and Where Are We Going: A Guide to Parish Planning.* New York: Sadlier, 1981.

St. Mary's Parish. *Ministry Booklet.* 1983. Available from P.O. Box H, Colts Neck, New Jersey 07722–0076.

Sloyan, Virginia, ed. *Touchstones for Liturgical Ministers.* Washington, D.C.: The Liturgical Conference, 1979.

Walters, Thomas P., ed. *Handbook for Parish Evaluation.* New York: Paulist Press, 1984.

Wilson, Marlene. *How to Mobilize Church Volunteers.* Minneapolis: Augsburg House, 1983.

Chapter 8

THE PEOPLE: WITHOUT WHOM, NOTHING

The group that benefits most from good leadership is the people. The parishioners help influence and shape the parish's liturgies, programs, and activities. They may not be aware of this influence, but their behavior, comments, and reactions affect parish priorities and planning. If one adult religious education program draws few people and another two hundred, which program will be repeated and which one dropped? If one type of song creates a good congregational response and another only silence, which song will be used again? If one youth activity results in ten letters of praise from parents and another ten letters of complaints, which one will be expanded and which cut back?

Obviously, the parish is not run in response to popular opinion. But the desires and expectations of the people do contribute to the goals and priorities of organizations and programs. The parishioners, in other words, are an integral part of leadership patterns in a parish. People also adjust to new shifts and emphases introduced by parish leaders. Contrary to comments we often hear from pastors and staffs, parishioners do change their opinions and expectations. The myth that Catholics resist change is not supported by our research on Catholic parishes.

Concerning liturgy, for instance, favorable attitudes towards the greeting of peace, lay ministers of Communion, and Communion in the hand have increased significantly over the last six years. In one parish the pastor and staff introduced a communal penance service after the last Mass on the first Sunday of every month. The service caught on. When we surveyed attitudes in that parish, we discovered that positive attitudes towards the communal penance service were 34 percent more than the typical response of 52 percent we receive for this question on our Parish Evaluation Project surveys, demonstrating that people change in response to the leaders' efforts.[1]

Change in the Parish

Like other groups, Catholic parishioners welcome change if certain conditions are present. First, if people see the change as inevitable, they adapt in order to meet the challenge. It is to their advantage to do so: the conditions won't change, so they change instead. This is how people react to growing older. Nothing can stop the process, so they adapt to meet the challenge. Parishioners react the same way toward changes in the parish. The roof collapses after a storm; the people respond with donations of time and money to meet the emergency. The associate pastor is not replaced, and the parish is left with only one priest; the people adapt to necessary changes in the Mass schedule.

A second condition percipitating change is present whenever people perceive some reward or advantage as a result of the change. If people think they will get something in return, they are more likely to take the risk of changing. For example, a person will shift financial investments hoping to reap a benefit in the future. A couple will take out a loan for a new house, knowing it will limit their spending money but feeling that the rewards are worth the change. The same is true in a parish. People are willing to risk becoming involved in teaching religious education classes or visiting shut-ins if they feel they will gain something from the experience; that is, if they see others enjoying this ministry, they want to be part of the experience. Again, if a pastor suggests a parish center as a new addition, the people contribute generously if they can realize—or be helped to realize—how much they will benefit from the new facility.

Third, people are also receptive to change if they have the tools, equipment, or training necessary for making the change. For example, people will risk a change of occupation or career if they have the necessary skills for the new job or at least know those skills can be easily acquired. Again, people will buy a home computer if the operating instructions can be followed easily.

Too often people resist change in a parish, however, because they are given a job to do with little or no training. They react against changes in the Mass, for instance, because they have not been given enough explanation about what the changes will entail or how to adapt to the new procedures. Changes as simple as receiving Communion in a new way, taking the Communion cup, answering prayers, or singing responses, if not adequately explained, will alienate people and even keep some from coming back to church.

In our parish survey, we ask people the reason they do not come to parish activities, and 20 percent respond that the primary reason is that they don't feel qualified to attend.[2] They don't have the necessary tools, in other words, and are fearful of new procedures.

Fourth, people change if they feel that the change is taking place in a supportive, friendly environment. When the atmosphere is one of "Everybody is doing it. Come on in, the water's fine," people will become part of the new routine or practice. Both young and old people follow current trends and fads in clothing, entertainment, recreation, and personal habits. Both the mass media and advertising use peer pressure techniques to introduce a wide variety of changes that people would not ordinarily undertake.

In a parish setting parishioners are likely to be more receptive to change if it is associated with a supported environment. The Rite of Christian Initiation for Adults (RCIA) helps those interested in the Catholic faith adjust to new ideas in a communal setting, supported by personal sponsors. These aspects of the initiation process make it a more friendly, manageable experience. Again, Mass-goers will participate in congregational song if others around them are singing. Volunteer singers distributed throughout the congregation influence more people to sing. Joining in doesn't become awkward or difficult. Soon the entire church is singing because of the subtle but effective support of the volunteer singers.

People will change, and even welcome change, when the four conditions of change—inevitability, promise of reward, preparation, and support—are present.[3] When church leaders say that they feel parishioners resist change, they are, in fact, admitting that one or more of the conditions for change have not been met. Sometimes parishioners are given the impression that a change is but a passing fancy of the present administration. ''Once the pastor leaves,'' they say, ''things will get back to normal again.'' They don't see the change as inevitable, only as a temporary inconvenience. Leaders must be careful, therefore, about the changes they introduce into the parish. For example, leaders should select a new hymnal with forethought and research because it will be used for years to come.

Parishioners also resist change if it holds out no rewards, if they are not given options or a trial period or a way to test the water and see that the change is an improvement. For example, if the music director decides to use a piano instead of an organ in church, the people may react badly if they feel that piano music is going to be forced down their throats. But if they realize some music is more prayerful, celebrative, and pleasant when played on the piano, they will be more open to this change. They will be even more open if given an option: the organ will be used for most hymns; the piano will be used for only two of the Masses on Sunday.

People dig in their heels when they hear about proposed changes in the parish if they don't have the tools or training necessary to deal with the change. They also react against those changes that occur in a nonsupportive, unfriendly environment. Small wonder people resist change when they are not given any preparation or support through the transition.

The same principles apply to parish leaders when they are asked to change. If a pastor, staff person, or council member is expected to change but is not given support, training, rewards, or an awareness of the necessity, then the person will fight the change, either directly or through passive resistance. Finally, successful leaders must recognize that in some parishes, the parishioners are more progressive than the leaders. Parishioners may demand immediate and far-ranging changes without really appreciating what the change will cost the leadership or recognizing that leaders may need time to adjust to new approaches and emphases. In other words, parishioners must apply to their leaders these four conditions for change in the same way that leaders must apply them to the people.

Hindrances to Parish Involvement

Most parish leaders would like to see a greater number of parishioners becoming involved in parish ministries, organizations, and programs. One of the primary benefits of restructuring the parish around a Pastoral Council of Ministries is that it opens up new avenues and possibilities for parishioner involvement. In a typical Catholic parish less than 40 percent participate in parish life beyond attending the weekend Masses, and less than 20 percent attend parish functions, other than the weekend Masses, once a month or more often.[4] Why is this percentage so small? Because there are so many obstacles to people's involvement in the parish. We can name and deal with these obstacles by grouping them into four categories built around the four aspects of leadership: leader, people, environment, and spirit.

In subtle and unconscious ways, parish leaders themselves contribute to keeping people away. Inappropriate leadership styles, such as the telling or selling forms discussed in "Five Styles of Pastoring" in Chapter 2, alienate people, as does the laissez-faire style of leadership. Poor examples set by staff, council, or commission members also keep people at a distance. Parishioners notice when the pastor and associate pastor are not giving each other support. They notice conflicts between the principal, youth director, and director of religious education. They witness vague, poorly run council meetings. They recognize heavy-handed tactics used by the Administration Commission or manipulative techniques used by the Community Life Commission. The people react by staying away. "Who needs the hassle?" they say to one another. "Those leaders are supposed to be living what they preach instead of arguing, bickering and backbiting."

Parishioner involvement is also affected by burnout among parish leaders. If someone comes to a pastor or staff member who is worn out from being spread out too thin, the leader may be unsympathetic or unresponsive. This is a serious problem for those in parish ministry. (We have addressed this in "Session 4: Handling Conflict" in Chapter 5.) Parish leaders must recognize that parishioners will hesitate to become involved in parish projects or ministries when their leaders are not relaxed or rested enough to direct the projects or ministries well.

Sometimes people's personal experience keeps them from being involved in the parish. Catholic parishioners are part of the American culture, which stresses individual expression and self-sufficiency. Mass media and advertising reinforce this individualism: it is better to have two or three cars in a family, so that every driver can be free to travel when and where he or she wishes; radios with headphones are a boon because they screen out distraction and leave the listener in a separate, independent world; townhouses and condominium complexes are often designed so that inhabitants can avoid the inconvenience of interacting with neighbors.

This trend toward privatism carries over into people's religious affiliation. Church becomes a Sunday (or Saturday night) experience. The rest of the people's lives is their own affair. Nothing or no one can intrude or penetrate this personal space. Thus, encouraging people to join parish groups or to participate in parish functions is met with resistance. Parishioners may satisfy their "obligations" (to attend Mass), but jealously protect the rest of their time.

The degree of parish involvement is also related to the recent proliferation of recreational and social outlets. Not many years ago people considered their parish to be the center of their lives. It was more than a Mass-on-Sunday experience. The parish was dances, ice-cream socials, bingo, sports, dinners, and parties besides. This is no longer the case. Most of these social outlets are satisfied through health clubs, sport leagues, hobbies, and recreational centers. What little time is left over from work and family is often given to activities and groups not associated with the parish.

People's experience also has demonstrated that parish involvement is often more than meets the eye. Put simply, some people decide to volunteer for what looks like a limited parish activity and soon discover that it is a time-consuming ministry instead. Parishioners sense that there is a catch to participation in parish projects and programs. They are afraid that once they volunteer, they will be called on to be part of parish functions every night of the week. Because they are afraid of becoming overextended, people don't volunteer at all.

Environmental obstacles also hinder people's involvement in parish functions. People hesitate to attend because the meetings take place at bad times or in poor locations. One experience of a dirty classroom with small desks and uncomfortable chairs becomes one experience too many. One Mass in the gymnasium or outdoors, at which people can't hear the readings or homily, the temperature is over eighty degrees, children are screaming, and the music is too loud is enough to keep even the most committed from coming back. One meeting in a home at which more attention is given to showing off the house than to dealing with the topic assures poor attendance for the next meeting.

The larger environment of the surrounding neighborhood also influences attendance. Parishes situated in high-crime areas have difficulty attracting people to the parish after dark. It is not the parish's fault, but it does affect parishioners' involvement. Parishes located in rural areas, in which people must travel long distances to get to church, are similarly hampered by the cost and inconvenience of traveling to the parish.

The size of the parish also affects involvement. No one likes to be lost in a cast of thousands. Large numbers of people attending church affect true participation. People need to be recognized, known by name, made to feel special, unique, and important. A parish congregation of a thousand or more families makes this difficult. "Why get involved?" people ask. "There are plenty of other folks. The parish doesn't need me."

Besides the hindrances associated with leaders, with people, and with environment, there are also hindrances related to the spirit of the parish. A poor image influences involvement. No one wants to be associated with a losing team. If rumors circulate about the poor reputation of the parish, people tend to shy away from becoming identified or associated with it. Poor publicity about past or present conflicts affects the people's level of commitment and participation. The growing shortage of priests can also affect the spirit of a parish. People become discouraged and fearful if they think theirs will be the next parish to close or to be reduced to the status of a mission with no resident pastor. Interestingly, however, this crisis can be used to strengthen the spirit of the parish community if it is dealt with in a creative manner.

Parish leaders should be aware that even little things such as the weather or the seasons of the year can put a damper on parish spirit. For example, it is easier to get people to volunteer for projects in September or October than it is in January or February. People tend to feel more positive about themselves and the parish when the weather is pleasant or when they have just returned from vacation.

Ways to Increase Parish Involvement

For each of the four aspects of leadership—leader, people, environment, and spirit—there are appropriate ways to increase the level of people's involvement. Parish leaders who practice an enabling, empowering style of facilitating leadership give people both the ability and the power to take ownership of parish ministries, projects and organizations. Providing a good example or model of cooperation and mutual support is also essential. The emphasis is not on leading so much as on living out the commitment to Christian community in one's everyday ministry.

Leaders must gather information about the needs, expectations and desires of the people they serve. They can then shape liturgies, programs, and group activities to fit the parishioners rather than force the people to adjust to prearranged schedules and agenda. Leaders should organize programs well, prepare far in advance but be ready to adjust to changing situations, run meetings efficiently, and help people feel that they have accomplished something by coming. The participants should not be kept beyond the appointed time for ending. A well-organized ministry with efficiently run meetings is a necessary ingredient for a high level of involvement.

Leaders should also overcommunicate parish events. The more important the occasion, the more often and the more varied the announcement of the event to the people should be. One notice in one medium is not enough. Posters, letters, bulletin notices, personal contacts, and phone calls should all be used to advertise important events in the parish. Notices in the bulletin or announcements from the pulpit are not enough to attract people. People must be contacted personally so that they feel their presence is important. A phone call reaps more results than a month-long campaign of written requests.

Parishioners respond best when parish functions relate to their self-interest and touch their lives, raise their curiosity, or promise to help them in their daily lives. Besides tapping self-interest, leaders must also be sensitive to special needs, such as child-care needs, handicaps, language difficulties, driving home through traffic. If parishioners experience awareness, sensitivity, and care for their needs, they will probably return for another session.

People are more likely to participate in a program that has an announced ending date and time. Signing up for three meetings over the next two months is less intimidating than committing oneself to a meeting every month for an indefinite period. Asking for a limited commitment attracts many more respondents than a call for volunteers that provides no indication of how much time is required. A time and talent search that asks people to sign up for activities and ministries in the parish meets with more success if the sign-up sheet specifies how many hours a month each activity requires.

Finally, leaders should not be afraid to challenge people to become involved and to hold them accountable to this commitment. If people feel called to be more creative, more insightful, and more energetic than they thought possible, they become pleased with themselves as they rise to meet the challenge. It tests their abilities and recognizes them as gifted, qualified adults. If they are also subject to periodic evaluations of their work, they begin to appreciate how important their contribution is. They grow to expect praise for their successes and supportive criticism of their less successful work.

Improving the environment and the spirit of the group also helps increase participation. For instance, a warm, inviting meeting area fosters a positive attitude among the participants. Providing rewards also keeps people interested and involved. These rewards might come from group interaction: receiving support for efforts, being able to share personal feelings and stories, or discovering the possibility of developing a new friendship. Other rewards include refreshments, music, entertainment, humor, and take-home materials. If people sense the environment is rewarding and that being part of a particular activity produces something worthwhile, then the word will get around and this activity will become popular.

An environment rich in symbols and visual displays creates a positive feeling among the participants. Liturgies enhanced with flowers, banners, music, and pageantry draw the largest attendance. Large parish gatherings that include the use of overhead projectors, charts, pictures, demonstrations, or role playing stir interest to a greater extent than do lectures or speeches.

Spiritual leaders should also appeal to a greater power—that is, to God—for recruiting parishioners. Emphasize a call to ministry and the opportunity to use one's gifts and talents in return for God's blessings. This is more likely to attract volunteers than an appeal such as, "We need more people to teach religious education classes. We're short two teachers." Leaders should instead ask people to search their hearts and see if the Spirit is calling them to something special this year, perhaps to use their abilities in helping the young learn about their faith. In this care it is Spirit with a capital S that is emphasized.[5]

Stressing the Spirit helps parishioners become aware of the death-resurrection cycle. Some aspects of parish life may be dying while others are rising to new life. Parish life is never on an even keel; it always has its peaks and valleys. Helping people appreciate this cycle of success and failure frees them from feeling that they have to be perfect to volunteer or that the activity must always be successful. It is sufficient to do what one can and to let the Spirit supply what is lacking. Lowering expectations reduces the pressure on volunteers and produces a more realistic frame of mind.

It is also important to acknowledge and build on whatever degree of success is achieved in a parish project or ministry. Emphasizing successful ventures helps create a positive spirit among those involved and improves the image the activity has in the parish as a whole. If a Lenten series works, broadcast it. If a music group or choir does a good job, praise them. If a program draws a large crowd, spread the word. If a special collection goes over the top, publicize it. An emphasis on success does wonders to attract a high level of involvement.

Finally, a crisis can draw people out of the woodwork and into the mainstream of parish life. We don't suggest that leaders create a crisis just to raise the energy level of the parishioners. But when one does occur, do use it creatively to build up the spirit of identity and sharing in the parish community. If the pastor gets laryngitis and can't do anything more than mouth the words at Mass, rally the congregation to speak the words of the eucharistic prayer along with him. If a storm causes a blackout during an important parish gathering, break out the candles and hold a prayer service for those who live without the light of Christ. If enrollment in the school drops below the level necessary to maintain it, gather the parishioners together to pray for insight into what God wishes for the future of the school and parish. A crisis, in other words, can either be a disaster that creates havoc or a moment of opportunity that raises the spirit of the people beyond anyone's expectations. A crisis can be an occasion for new growth rather than a time of devastation to be avoided at all costs.

Three Successful Parishes

St. Brigid's is close to the center of the city. It used to have a large parish plant, including a church, convent, rectory, and school. All these buildings are gone. What has taken their place is a small building used for a variety of events. The rest of the property was sold to make room for an attractive, low-income housing complex.

The assets from this sale of property helped finance the parish center. This income was supplemented by donations from a number of wealthier parishes, who volunteered not only money but also time and talent to help the two hundred black and Hispanic parishioners put up an efficient, low-cost, multipurpose building. During the week the building is used as a day-care facility for working parents. In the evening it becomes a meeting place for small groups. On Sunday it is the worship space for the parish community.

Most of the small groups that meet in the evenings are faith-sharing groups that concentrate on community building, story telling, and personal problem solving. These groups form the basis of people's association with the parish. The gatherings include prayer, scriptural reading, and reflection on how the Gospels are lived out in one's daily life.

Only one Mass is held in the parish center each week. Because the community is a mixture of both black and Hispanic cultures, the flavor of the Sunday morning Mass alternates between black and Hispanic customs and preferences. Once a month the two cultures are combined in a single liturgy. There is no resident priest in the parish. Instead, three priests who live communally in another parish share the responsibility for Mass and Sacraments at St. Brigid's.

The daily operation of the parish is handled by parishioners who volunteer their services for a two-month commitment. These volunteers are coordinated by two part-time staff members, an Hispanic permanent deacon and a black woman who is parish minister. The planning of Sunday liturgies, the organization of small groups, the lifelong education program, and the outreach ministry are all handled by parish volunteers.

The biggest obstacle the parish had to overcome was the mixture of black and Hispanic cultures. Both groups had their own expectations for liturgy, music, and parish celebrations. Even talking about common concerns and problems was difficult because they did not always understand each other or talk the same language. Slowly they worked out their differences as both groups realized that there was room for their own individual needs and ways of praying, worshiping, and socializing. They also discovered that both groups had many common cares, concerns, and insights that helped them work together on parish projects and programs.

The parish operates a school that serves the larger community. Only one-third of the students are Catholic. The rest come from families who pay extra so their children can attend the school because it provides quality education and a better environment for learning and value formation. The tuition, of course, does not provide enough to meet expenses. To offset these expenses, three other parishes in the diocese contribute to the upkeep of the school as a ministry of outreach of service.

This inner-city parish has its own unique character and style. It also makes a significant contribution to the larger Catholic church. The parish belongs to the people. It finds its energy in the small group faith-sharing communities. It incorporates within its identity a variety of cultures, expectations, and needs. It is alive to the Spirit in its midst. In these ways it is an example to the rest of the diocese and the Church as a whole of what a parish with limited financial resources can be.

St. Thomas More Parish is located in an affluent suburb. It has a large plant that includes a church, school, convent, and rectory. Only the church is presently used as was originally intended, and that with major renovations.

The school building is now a combination youth center and religious education complex for all ages. The rectory has been made into an administration center, which includes offices for the staff and parish volunteers, a parish computer network, and communication/publications operations. The two priests on staff live in a house a few blocks from church. They made this move last year and are learning to cook and keep house. They were challenged by others on the staff to try this out as an experiment. So far, what they have lost in convenience they feel they have gained in distance. They no longer feel pressured by the proximity of work and living space.

The convent has been made into a recollection/retreat center; it includes prayer rooms, chapel, and conference space. The church building itself is flexible so that on Sunday morning it can accommodate a congregation of two thousand for Mass, but by evening it can be set up for a lecture series, and on the next day it can seat a thousand people for a parish buffet and social.

The parish staff consists of two priests, one nun, one deacon, and three full-time professional ministers. The parish numbers just over two thousand persons. The priests act as co-pastors. They share their role equally, although one is responsible for administrative tasks and the other for liturgical planning. With the help of the staff, each has drawn up a job description that describes not only his pastoral duties but also his responsibilities as a member of the parish staff.

The staff itself has asked a facilitator to help it work better as a team. This has improved the level of interaction and the staff members feel they are now providing a better service to the parish as a whole. One woman minister on staff is in charge of the retreat center. It is used every day for prayer groups, scriptural reading, liturgical services, and days of recollection. A number of parishioners have been trained as counselors and spiritual directors so that the many people who come to the parish for direction can be accommodated. All the adults in the parish are encouraged to talk over their faith journey in a group or with a director at least once a month.

The emphasis in the parish is on everyday ministry. Parishioners are encouraged to look at their own occupations to see how these can be considered as a ministry. How does a doctor, nurse, salesperson, or government employee become an on-the-job minister? People of similar professions come together to talk about their work and discover how they can become more caring, sensitive, and Christian people. Most of the parishioners commit themselves not only to contributing a percentage of their income to the ministries of the parish and Church, but also to a limited period of service as a parish worker. They spend time helping out either at the weekend Masses, the retreat center, the educational/youth complex, or in the administration/communication ministry.

The communication ministry is what makes the rest of the parish operation possible. This is the full-time ministry of one of the staff members. At the core of this ministry is a communication network that links all parishioners through the use of a parish computer. The people are kept informed of current parish events, financial contributions, areas that need attention, and ministries that could use more volunteers. The computer also makes it possible to send out monthly "probe cards," which ask for feedback about various events and emphases in the parish. Special interest groups are given unique attention, as are newcomers to the parish. Each parishioner feels that he or she is not just a number in the files, but someone who is special, with unique interests, capabilities, talents, and expectations.

Of special note is that St. Thomas More Parish is successful because its primary focus is lifelong conversion. Although much of the people's social and family lives are lived out in places independent of the parish, people learn the meaning of life and their response to God's call through their involvement and association with the parish, which in turn helps to shape the rest of their lives.

Sacred Heart Parish is located in a small town with a population of less than a thousand people. The parish is half that size, drawing members from the surrounding area. It has been functioning for the last five years without a resident priest—and functioning well. The parishioners were at first angry and confused when they lost their priest-pastor. The bishop gave them only two alternatives: close down or accept a nun as their pastor. The parishioners decided to give Sister Marion a try. Although they joke about it now, in the beginning it was tough going for everyone. It took about a year before the people and Sister Marion got used to one another.

Presently, Sacred Heart parishioners celebrate Mass only twice a month. On interim Sundays they celebrate a community-run worship service, with readings, shared reflections, and a Communion service. These services have become the high point of the week for the entire parish. Everyone takes part in the music, shared prayer, and reflections.

The biweekly Mass pulls in people from all around, especially from the neighboring town in which Sacred Heart's sister parish is located. The breakfast that follows Mass lasts all morning. Parishioners, of course, are free to attend the sister parish on alternate Sundays if they want to attend Mass more often, but most prefer their own worship services.

Sacred Heart is known for its outreach ministry. When Sister Marion Kenny came as the resident pastor, she brought with her an interest in social justice issues. Knowing that she had to win over the hearts of the people, she did not at first share her concerns for the poor and alienated. She waited for almost two years.

But when parishioners became upset about the deteriorating condition of their land and the threat of losing their farms to large corporations, she helped them form a cooperative that prevented outside groups from manipulating them and taking over their farmlands. This experience helped the people become more sensitive to others in need. Some of the parishioners discovered a group of migrant workers who lived in poor and unhealthy conditions. Sister Marion not only helped the parishioners to provide better housing for the migrant workers, but also challenged them to reflect on their own lives to see if a simpler way of life might not bring more meaning and happiness to their own families. Slowly, the social consciousness of the people developed so that when the bishop asked for volunteers to confront government agencies on issues related to peace and justice, the parishioners from Sacred Heart responded in large numbers.

If in the future the Church rewrites its laws to allow women to be ordained, the only change this would mean for Sacred Heart Parish is that the people would be able to celebrate Mass on a more regular basis. Sister Marion could easily fill the role of priest-pastor. She has completed the necessary training and has all the needed experience. Ordination would only ratify the role of pastor she has already been exercising.

These are but three scenarios of successful parishes in the American Catholic Church. Many stories could be told about other parishes responding to unique and demanding situations. These stories amply prove that such successes are possible in today's Church; the seeds for growth and vitality are already sown. We have witnessed these seeds being planted, watered, and given sunlight in many places across the country. We have no doubt that the Spirit is alive and working in our American Catholic Church today. It will be an exciting experience to watch these parishes grow into adulthood in the years to come.

The Essentials of Being a Parish

We have come a long way from the somewhat discouraging parish scenario of Chapter 1. We have looked at the history of parish, described the essentials of good leadership, and shown how good leadership affects the roles of pastor, staff, council, commissions, and people. The underlying theme that has permeated this book is that a parish cannot be a success without good leadership. Good leadership hinges on the following six ingredients:

1. A facilitating style of leadership by pastor, staff, and parish leaders. The old practice of simply making decisions and then announcing or selling them to the parishioners is being met with less and less acceptance. Working *with* rather than *for* the people is the most effective means of good leadership.
2. Constant reference to the Spirit, the Gospels, and the creative power of God in our midst. Becoming a successful parish is far beyond the capabilities of leaders or people. Only God can make a successful parish. The role of leader is to be co-worker with this loving God.
3. Leaders working in collaboration. St. Paul's image of the Church as a body, with its many unique and varied functions

coordinated for the single purpose of life, is an appropriate model for parish life. The pastor, staff, and leaders must strive to work as a team rather than a collection of individual ministers. Each person's gifts and talents contribute to the overall effort of building up the parish community.

4. Leaders who enable and empower parishioners. Both enabling and empowering are necessary. The leaders must support, challenge, train, and encourage people to fulfill their unique call to ministry. But the leaders must also step back and give people the freedom, initiative, and power to make decisions within their own sphere of operation and influence. Good leadership, therefore, means letting the people be the co-owners, co-leaders, co-workers, and co-ministers in the parish, in service to one another and to the broader community.

5. Adequate organization and structures that allow the parish to maintain a high level of shared ministry and involvement with a minimum of strife and conflict. A successful parish is not a simple operation, but a complex mixture of relationships, group interaction, and mutual accountability. Because the parish is complex, it needs a structure that allows for new avenues of growth and expansion as well as stability and continuity. The role of leadership is to match parish needs with a structure and style of operation that provide an adequate response to these needs.

The parish as a whole is made up of more than its leadership. What are the essentials of being a parish? They hinge on the two commandments of Jesus: love of God and love of neighbor. All who follow Jesus are called to live out these two commandments in their daily lives. Unfortunately, many elements in American culture work against these laws of love. The emphasis on self-sufficiency lends itself to mistrust of others and self-involvement: "Don't rely on anyone else, except as a means for becoming a success or acquiring more possessions or exercising more power. Worship yourself and your own way of life." As for loving others, our culture considers this a sign of weakness: "Love another in a romantic way, but when this loving is no longer self-serving, find someone else." And as for loving other people who might be in need, our culture tells us that this is not worth the risk: "Watch out! You might get hurt, robbed, even killed if you open up too much to the poor and needy."

Such stress on individualism is only one aspect of American culture, but it is a strong one. Individuals find it difficult to resist the lure to serve oneself before all others, God included. This is where the parish comes into play. A successful parish is a gathering of people, drawn together around the two communal expressions of loving God and loving neighbor. In the parish community these two commandments or expressions are called *worship* and *ministry*.

The parish community helps people find God, love God, worship God. This is much more than a one-hour-per-weekend experience. It permeates the entire life of the parish. Finding God includes eucharistic worship, sacraments, education, Scripture, small groups, organizations, all that goes into life-long conversion and the journey of faith.

The parish community also helps people minister, both to one another and to those beyond the parish membership. Being a minister is a scary and sometimes lonely experience. It requires group support, communal discernment, personal invitation, and direct challenge. In short, ministering needs a parish to make it work. This is not to say that ministering always takes place within the context of parish life and structures. In fact, most ministering takes place in people's everyday lives of work, family, and relationships. But a parish is necessary as a place to foster social awareness, provide options and insights, give training, share experiences, discern new directions, and link individual efforts to the larger mystery of being a follower of Christ.

The essential nature of a parish is to provide the occasion and opportunity for people to find God (worship) and to share God with others (ministry). It is up to parish leadership to allow this and to facilitate it. The leadership task in a successful parish is much like that described in St. Paul's letter to the Christian community in Thessalonica:

Live together in peace, and our instruction to this end is to reprimand the unruly, encourage the timid, help the weak and be very patient with all men [and women].

Be sure that no one repays a bad turn by a bad turn; good should be your objective always, among yourselves and in the world at large.

Be happy in your faith at all times. Never stop praying. Be thankful, whatever the circumstances may be.

If you follow this advice you will be working out the will of God to you expressed in Christ Jesus.

Never damp the fire of the Spirit, and never despise what is spoken in the name of God. By all means use your judgment, and hold on to whatever is really good. Steer clear of evil in any form.

May the God of peace make you holy through and through.

1 Thessalonians 5:14–23.[6]

NOTES

1. Parish Evaluation Project, *A Survey of Parish Attitudes and Practices,* Rev. Ed. (Chicago: Parish Evaluation Project, 1985), p. 2.
2. Ibid., p. 8.
3. These categories of change are described in David Pearce Snyder, "Social, Economic, and Technological Trends and Developments that Will Reshape America during the Next Ten Years." Speech delivered at the Great Lakes Pastoral Ministries Gathering, Des Plaines, IL, 1983. Available on tape from *National Catholic Reporter.*
4. Parish Evaluation Project, *A Survey of Parish Attitudes and Practices,* p. 1–3.
5. For a checklist on how to recruit volunteers and maintain their commitment, see Jackie McMakin, "How to Prevent Lay Leader Burnout," *Alban Institute Action Newsletter* 8 (January–February 1982): p. 1–3.
6. Quoted from J. B. Phillips, *The New Testament in Modern English* (New York: Macmillan, 1962).

Further Reading

Broholm, Dick, and John Hoffman. *Empowering Laity for Their Full Ministry: Nine Blocking Enabling Forces.* Newton Centre, Mass.; Andover Newton Laity Project, 1981.

Byers, David, ed. *The Parish In Transition: Proceedings of a Conference on the American Catholic Parish.* Washington, D.C.: United States Catholic Conference, 1986.

Chittister, Joan D., OSB, and Martin E. Marty, *Faith & Ferment.* Collegeville, Minn.: Liturgical Press, 1983.

Geaney, Dennis. *Full Church, Empty Rectory: Training Lay Ministers for Parishes Without Priests.* Notre Dame: Fides/Claretian, 1980.

Herr, Edward C., ed. *Tomorrow's Church*. Chicago: Thomas More Association, 1982.

Maney, Thomas. *Basic Communities: A Practical Guide for Renewing Neighborhood Churches*. Minneapolis: Winston Press, 1984.

Appendix

A CHECKLIST FOR WEEKEND LITURGIES

T he weekend liturgies are of critical importance to the life of a parish community. For most parishioners the one hour spent in church on Saturday evening or on Sunday is their only contact with the parish. The leadership must create liturgical celebrations that provide an atmosphere conducive to prayer and shared faith.

The following checklist offers a means of evaluating the weekend liturgies so that successful aspects can be reinforced and weak ones improved.

Individuals who plan and run the weekend liturgies fill out this checklist on their own and then bring the results to a group of five or six other liturgical ministers and planners to compare results. The checklist can also be used by the Worship and Spiritual Life Commission as a means of evaluating the weekend Masses. Those areas that scored high are acknowledged and reinforced. Those that scored low become the subject of future study and creative planning.

To use this checklist, assign a score of one (poor) to nine (excellent) to each aspect of the liturgy. There is no score of ten because that would mean that the ideal has been reached, and the ideal can never be attained.

Score:	1	3	5	7	9
	Poor	Fair	Average	Good	Excellent

Each of the following areas of the liturgy can be scored from one to nine on this scale.

Preparation

Good liturgy is the result of good planning. How well prepared are the weekend Masses? Is there a planning committee that prepares overall direction of the liturgies? Does the planning reflect the variety of people attending Mass? Is there room for those who like to pray quietly at Mass? Is there a Mass for young people? Are the various age, ethnic, and interest groups given attention in the selection of songs and responses? Is the music well prepared?

Have the lectors, servers, ushers, greeters, and choir been trained in advance so they know their roles and know how they fit into the larger goal of providing a good occasion for worship and communal prayer? Have all the people involved in the liturgical ministry spent time in preparing themselves and the area for which they are responsible before arriving at church on Sunday or Saturday evening?

Do those preparing the prayers, readings, songs, and responses pay attention to the use of balanced language, making sure that both feminine and masculine terms are used throughout the worship service? The Nicene Creed, for example, contains two phrases that could be changed in order to provide more balanced language: "for us men. . . " can be changed to "for us. . . " and ". . . became man" can be changed to ". . . became one of us."

Environment

Much of the success or failure of the weekend liturgies depends not on what is said or done during Mass, but upon the environment in which liturgy takes place. Is the place of worship kept clean? Are missalettes, song sheets, and envelopes neatly organized or scattered about? Is the church decorated to reflect the season, but not cluttered or filled with distracting symbols? Are the sound system, lighting, and temperature conducive to a prayerful and warm atmosphere so as not to distract from the Mass? Are the needs of special groups, such as ramps for the handicapped and special seating for the hard of hearing or invalids, taken into account? Are kneelers padded so that they don't bang when raised or lowered? Is the sanctuary well suited to provide a good focus for worship and prayer? Are different worship environments—the church building, a meeting room, or the outdoors—utilized for different needs, ages, and groups?

Music

Not all weekend Masses have music. Music may not be appropriate for the early Sunday Mass, for instance. Different styles of worship fit different types of congregations. For those Masses that include music, how well is it executed? Does the selection of songs fit the worshipers? Are the people well motivated so that they come to church looking forward to singing?

Music has a way of stirring peoples' hearts and providing a prayerful outlet and spiritual uplift not possible through words alone. But music done poorly can destroy the best intentions for worship and communal prayer. Does the choir or folk group inspire communal song, or does either get in the way of congregational singing? Is the accompaniment—organ, piano, guitar, flute—an asset or a production that draws attention to itself? Are solos tastefully done or are they a distraction to worship?

Gathering Rites

How are people welcomed as they come to Mass? Are there greeters at the door to convey a welcoming spirit when people enter the church? Is there a good balance between making people feel accepted and invited but not coerced or pressured? Do the ushers, in seating people, respect people's preferences, as well as encourage them to sit toward the front?

How do the priests and ministers enter the place of worship? The style of entrance, along with the music used, can set the mood of the Mass. Is the entrance warm, inviting, friendly? Or is it cool, aloof, and perfunctory?

How well are the first few moments of greeting and calling people to the presence of God used at your weekend Masses? How is the Penitential Rite conducted? Does it relate to people's daily lives? Are different forms used for different liturgical seasons? Does it help the congregation give thanks for blessings received and ask forgiveness for their failings?

Liturgy of the Word

A renewed emphasis on the Word is one result of the changes since the Second Vatican Council. Parishioners are more aware of the importance of Scripture and the proclamation of God's Word at Mass. As proof of this, when we ask people on our Parish Evaluation Project surveys the reason they attend Mass on the weekend, a higher percentage (40 percent) respond ''to hear the Word of God,'' rather than ''out of a sense of obligation'' (35 percent).[1]

How is the Liturgy of the Word celebrated in your parish? Is the Scripture read with understanding and care? Are people encouraged to listen intently and to allow God's Word to speak to their experience? Are missalettes used as a substitute for attentive listening? Is there time after each reading to let people reflect quietly on what it means for them? Are the people helped to understand the reason for the silence?

Is the sung (or spoken) response to the readings conducive to prayer and reflection, or has it become a habit that has little or no meaning? Does the Alleluia herald the Gospel, or has it become routine? If your parish has a Gospel procession, does it help people reverence the Word or merely provide an elaborate means of getting from the presiding chair to the pulpit?

Is there variety in the way the Word is presented at different Masses—multiple readers, special gestures, mime, audio visuals— so that the people remain aware of its freshness and significance in their daily lives? Are sound criteria employed for choosing a lector, along with periodic evaluations? Do the lectors gather for mutual support and affirmation? Are they thanked for the critical role they perform in the weekend liturgies?

The homily is meant to explicate the Word. This, of course, will vary depending on the person giving the homily. But as a whole, how well is the Word explained and applied to people's everyday lives? Does it hold people's interest? Does it relate to the various interests and backgrounds of the listeners? Does your parish encourage variety in the homilies? For example, the homilist might occasionally leave the pulpit and walk in front of the altar with a traveling microphone, or different people might speak at this time so that others besides the priest or deacon give reflections on the readings. (This is most appropriate for special occasions, such as Mother's Day, Father's Day, anniversaries, or feast days.)

In some parishes the priests and deacons have asked for help in preparing their homilies. Parishioners volunteer to meet with the homilist well in advance of the target weekend. They pray over the readings, reflect on key themes and passages, discuss how the Scripture is reflected in their daily lives, and suggest approaches and ideas for the coming homily. These homily groups need not meet every week; they could meet once a month or five weeks in a row twice a year. Homilists who have used this resource have found it a great help.

Other parishes have found periodic homily evaluations to be helpful. With the priests' or deacons' approval, people are called at random and asked what Mass they attend and whether they would be willing to stay after Mass one Sunday next month to provide feedback on the homily. When five volunteers have been recruited for each Mass, these people meet with someone other than the homilist after Mass. Each person fills out a card with five questions: (1) What was your general reaction toward the homily? (2) How well was the sermon delivered? That is, did it hold your interest? (3) Did the homily give you insights into the meaning of the Scriptures? (4) To what extent did the homily relate to your everyday life? (5) Are there any other comments you would like to make about the homily? The first four questions are rated on a scale from one to nine, poor to excellent. The last question is open-ended and allows people to give additional comments.

The volunteers are given a chance to voice their reactions in the group. The discussion is taped and, along with the survey cards, given to the homilist as a means of providing feedback and evaluation.

Transitional Rites

How well is the transition made from the Liturgy of the Word to the Liturgy of the Eucharist? These rites include the Profession of Faith, General Intercessions, and Preparation of Gifts.

Is the Nicene Creed introduced in such a way that it helps people reflect on the principles of their faith, or is it merely a recitation of rote phrases? Are alternative expressions of faith used on occasion to heighten awareness? These alternatives might include the Apostles' Creed or one created by the confirmation class or adult catechumens. Such a simple gesture as the presider pausing for a moment of silence and asking people to think of those aspects of their faith they treasure the most could create a new awareness of what the Profession of Faith entails.

How well are the General Intercessions (Prayers of the Faithful) done at your liturgies? Do they foster communal prayer or have they become an exercise that has lost significance? Are there a variety of methods used to encourage the spirit of prayer and petition among the parishioners? For example, some parishes use a petition book in which people write in the names of those needing prayers. The book is then placed on the altar during Mass. Other parishes print the names of the sick and deceased in the bulletin so that everyone can include these people in their prayers. Still other parishes include in the General Intercessions parish programs and special projects asking people to pray for the ministers and participants of these activities. Finally, some parishes provide the space and time for parishioners to contribute their own spontaneous prayers of petition as part of the General Intercessions.

As for the Preparation of Gifts, are the parishioners at your weekend Masses helped to understand the symbolic value, not only of the bread and wine, but of their money as well? Do they experience the collection as a gesture of returning to God a small share of the many riches showered upon them? Or is the predominant spirit one of restlessness while the congregation waits for the collection to be completed and the bread, wine, and collection basket brought to the altar?

Liturgy of the Eucharist

The Liturgy of the Eucharist begins with the Preface. This is the time at which everyone stands and acknowledges God as Savior, Redeemer, forgiver of sins, Spirit of life, and source of all goodness. Does the presider pray these prayers with the people, gathering together the prayers and aspirations of the congregation? Or are the Preface and Eucharistic Prayer recited as a routine exercise with little feeling or inspiration? Are the people given a chance to participate with the presider and make these prayers their own? For example, this can be accomplished by including quiet moments, adding special intentions, or responding in song and group prayer to the Preface, Institution Narrative, and Doxology.

Does the body language of the congregation add to the worshiping atmosphere? Simple gestures such as standing for the prayer, joining or lifting hands for the Lord's Prayer, or walking around the church for the peace greeting can help people feel a sense of community during the liturgy. These gestures may change for different Masses on the weekend, but they are critical for a greater sense of involvement and participation by the congregation. Without them, people become spectators, watching the "professionals" perform the service.

Is receiving Communion a prayerful experience for the congregation or one that is filled with confusion and consternation in getting to the Communion station and back to their seats? Is Communion under both species of bread and wine provided for those who wish it? Our surveys of parish attitudes show a rising concern among parishioners about the health risks of receiving wine from a common cup. Is there sensitivity among the leadership about this concern and an effort to provide alternative methods of receiving under both species of bread and wine for those who wish? Are eucharistic ministers given training and an appreciation of their servant role? In some parishes eucharistic ministers distribute Communion to the congregation before receiving themselves as a way of symbolizing their servant role.

Concluding Rites

Communion is not the end of the Mass, but it is often difficult to keep people from feeling that it is. Liturgical ministers need to reflect on how the last few moments of the liturgy can be used to best advantage.

Does the time after Communion provide an occasion for reflecting on God's special presence and how this presence is carried into a person's everyday life? If announcements are presented after Communion, are they given with tact and brevity so as not to distract from the spirit of the Mass?

In some parishes where the congregation is small, this time is also used for welcoming newcomers and congratulating those with birthdays and wedding anniversaries. This is done as a means of connecting the celebration of the Mass to people's daily lives.

The experience of worship does not end with the final song. It continues in the vestibule, parking lot, and over coffee and doughnuts in the parish hall. What do people encounter as they leave the church? Is it a pleasant farewell and an invitation to spend time in the church hall for refreshment and conversation? Or are people bombarded with raffle tickets, sign-up sheets, and hand-outs? Does your parish provide a balance in this regard so that parishioners do not become alienated by the pressure of too much thrown at them at once?

This period after Mass might also be the best occasion for short talks on prayer, moral or social issues, parenting, and Bible study. If Masses are schedule to allow more time between celebrations, people might be more willing to stay afterwards and gain much through the experience. Adult faith development programs after Mass, if approached with creativity and sensitivity to people's needs and desires, can improve the tone of the liturgies themselves.

How well does your parish maintain the spirit of worship and community building during the Concluding Rites, both while in church and immediately following Mass? Is time well used, or are people ushered out and then left to their own devices? Some parishioners prefer to be left alone after Mass. Others are lonely and would enjoy a little time for interaction. Are allowances made for both responses?

Add up your score on your checklist. The highest possible score is 72. If yours is above 60, count your blessings. A score of 56 is good, and 40 is average. Compare your score with the score of other liturgical ministers or with the score of the Worship and Spiritual Life Commission. Look at the aspects of the Mass that received the highest scores and congratulate yourselves for a job well done. Look at the aspects that received low scores and devote more attention toward improving these areas for the coming year.

NOTES

1. Parish Evaluation Project, *A Survey of Parish Attitudes and Practices*, Rev. Ed. (Chicago: Parish Evaluation Project, 1985), p. 8.

The Parish Evaluation Project (PEP) provides services to individual parishes over an extended period of time (usually from two to three years) to help them in needs assessment, goal setting, leadership training, staff development, and evaluation techniques. PEP also provides resources to staffs, lay leaders, diocesan agencies, and religious organizations in many areas related to pastoral ministry and leadership. Further information is available from the Parish Evaluation Project, 1307 S. Wabash Avenue, Suite 203, Chicago, IL 60605, (312) 427-4392.

INDEX